The BEATS ABROAD

A Global Guide to the Beat Generation

Bill Morgan

City Lights Books San Francisco

For Oliver Sacks, who, like the Beat writers,
found his inspiration in the people of the world

Library of Congress Cataloging-in-Publication Data
Morgan, Bill, 1949–
 The Beats abroad : a global guide to the Beat Generation / Bill
Morgan.
     pages cm
 ISBN 978-0-87286-689-8 (paperback)
 1. Beat generation—Travel. 2. Literary landmarks. 3. Authors,
American—20th century—Travel. I. Title.
 PS228.B6M576 2015
 810.9'0054—dc23
                                        2015026728

City Lights Books are published at the City Lights Bookstore,
261 Columbus Avenue, San Francisco, CA 94133.
Visit our website: www.citylights.com

CONTENTS

INTRODUCTION

When City Lights published the third in this series of Beat guidebooks in 2011, I felt it might be the final one. By then I had tracked the writers of the Beat Generation through their haunts in New York City, San Francisco, and all the fifty states. It wasn't until fans asked for specific information about sites in Paris, Mexico City, and Tangier that I realized there was one more guide to create, an international one. Although it wasn't intentional, the publication of this fourth book also rounds out a rough chronological survey of the Beat movement itself. During the 1940s and 1950s, the writers we think of as "beat" first became friends in New York City. In the mid-fifties they joined other writers in San Francisco to form the group that came to be known as the "Beat Generation." By the 1960s their books had become well-known throughout the United States and served as seminal texts for the youth counterculture that was emerging. The final dissemination of their works was international and began in the later sixties, a diaspora that continues to this very day. Many of these writers developed international reputations, as translations of their works found publishers around the world from China to South Africa. Globally there were surprises. Translations of Bob Kaufman's poetry made him more popular in France than he was in America. Although he considered himself to be French as a boy, Lawrence Ferlinghetti's fame in Italy continues to grow. Ginsberg's work has always enjoyed a wide audience throughout Eastern Europe, where the communist governments mistakenly believed his anti-capitalist stance made him their ally. And to this day nearly every bookstore in Rome carries a large selection of Kerouac titles, often displayed on the most prominent tables in the front of the shops.

This volume documents that final international

phase of the Beat Generation's story in three ways. First and foremost, it identifies specific places where the Beats hung out. Second, it shows how the Beat Generation influenced the work of authors in those countries. And finally, it shows by example the tremendous influence that international travel had on these writers.

The earliest international traveler was Lawrence Ferlinghetti. Due to a strange twist of fate that will be explained later, Ferlinghetti was taken to France as a baby and raised there until the age of five. William S. Burroughs, the oldest of the core group of Beat writers, was the first one to voluntarily decide to live abroad. Never truly comfortable in the States, he moved to Vienna following his graduation from Harvard in 1936. He planned to continue his studies in an Austrian medical school, but stayed only one term. During that period he sampled the independence and liberation that life as an expatriate offered him. When Burroughs eventually returned to America, he brought with him a bit of the polished continental lifestyle that his younger friends found charming and seductive a decade later.

In 1949 Burroughs left the country again and lived abroad for the next twenty-five years. He was followed by the others: Ginsberg, Corso, Kerouac, Orlovsky, and Ansen, who all traveled to Europe and North Africa in part to follow in Burroughs' footsteps. Later Snyder, Whalen, Kyger, and Waldman would each spend time in Asia, while McClure, Jones, Bremser, Ferlinghetti, Lamantia, and Cassady fell under the spell of Mexico as well as Central and South America. The Beat writers appeared at countless international poetry festivals over the years, and in the course of their travels, they influenced a new generation of writers. Each incorporated their travel experiences into their writing, reacting to the new surroundings. As they grew older and visited more widely, their own opinions about the world changed. Burroughs hated everything about Italy on his first trip, but mellowed with time. Ginsberg, perhaps the most widely traveled, was changed dramatically by the two years he spent in India, but later in life was reluctant to make the trip again when he had the chance. Initially Kerouac found Mexico magical, but on later trips he grew disappointed by the changes he found there. Each had his or her own adventures "on the road" abroad, and this book will guide the reader who wants to follow in the footsteps of the Beats worldwide.

The book is arranged geographically by continent, country, and city. No attempt has been made to be comprehensive in coverage. Including every town each visited would be overwhelming and unrewarding, for the range of their travels was encyclopedic. Locations were selected based on their importance to authors' writings and biographies. The fact that Ginsberg and Burroughs read in Finland was not in itself important enough to merit inclusion, but the fact that Corso had a mystical vision on the island of Hydra, or that Kerouac wrote *Doctor Sax* in a room on Orizaba Street in Mexico City makes those places essential to the Beat story.

Allen Ginsberg in particular seems to have visited every country on earth during his reading tours, and listing every one of those places would be pointless. Gregory Corso probably stayed in more than a hundred apartments in Paris and Rome alone, and citing each address would be futile. Even Kerouac, who traveled abroad less than others, passed through dozens of Mexican towns on trips to and from Mexico City, often mentioning them in his prose. Only the more important locations have been described in the pages that follow. And so, for the fourth and final time, grab your passport and follow along.

I

FRANCE
AND
MEDITERRANEAN
EUROPE

PARIS

The city of Paris was one of the central ports of call for the members of the Beat Generation during the middle of the twentieth century. Not only did they find the literary and artistic heritage of the city inspiring, but the pace of life was more to their liking, as was the relative freedom they enjoyed. A few of the Beat writers visited Paris in their youth, but most came as young adults, lured by the carefree lifestyle and more liberal drug policies that had been glamorized by the writers of the Lost Generation. We begin with two locations that will feature in many of the stories to follow, and then move on through the authors and their Parisian adventures.

1. The Beat Hotel. The legendary hotel at **9, rue Gît-le-Cœur**, in Paris's Latin Quarter, deserves an entry all its own. For thirty years, beginning in 1933, the manager, bartender, and concierge of the building was Madame Rachou, a woman who enjoyed the company of writers and artists and made allowances for them when they were financially down on their luck. Although the forty-two-room hotel never actually had a name, so many of the writers of the Beat Generation stayed here between 1958 and 1963 that it became widely known as "The Beat Hotel." The rooms were tiny, dark cells; each floor shared a single dingy bathroom; the heat and electricity were sporad-

Gregory Corso at the Beat Hotel, 1957–58

ic, and the walls so thin that residents could hear their neighbors breathing. The low rent and the landlady's permissive attitude were ideal for poverty-stricken writers. William Burroughs, Gregory Corso, Allen Ginsberg, Peter Orlovsky, and Harold Norse all made it their home, and nearly every one of our writers, with the exception of Jack Kerouac, stayed here at some point.

Madame Rachou closed the hotel in 1963, and her Beat tenants, unable to afford the higher rents imposed by the new owners, found lodgings elsewhere. Harold Norse's eulogy for the hotel, "The Death of 9, Rue Gît-Le-Cœur," appeared in the first issue of *City Lights Journal*. In it, on the eve of the hotel's renovation, he describes the habitual goings-on: "dreamachine spins round & round opening up hash visions & colors as it crashes the sight barrier & changes cells of the brain . . . a great American writer receives whole episodes in his sleep for the novel of the century . . . a poem like a BOMB goes off. " But then he goes on: "the hotel has changed hands. Workmen hammer & plaster, halls full of tools & bags of cement, old spiral staircase white with dust. No more all night jam sessions under ceilings about to fall, cats on the floor in sleeping-bags, eight or nine to a pad. No more guitars & horns." Although it is still a hotel today, it has been greatly gentrified and only the exterior walls remain as they were during its Beat heyday.

2. Shakespeare and Company. For more than sixty years, the English-language bookstore founded by George Whitman at **37, rue de la Bûcherie** has attracted Beat authors and their fans on visits to Paris. Founded in August 1951 as the Mistral Bookshop, the store was renamed "Shakespeare and Company" a decade later, after the famous Parisian bookstore that first published James Joyce's *Ulysses*. Whitman got his start in the book business by selling textbooks to American students at the

Sorbonne, and one of his earliest customers was Lawrence Ferlinghetti—the two were to become lifelong friends. Once he'd opened up his bookstore, George was not content to merely operate a commercial business, and he made the shop into a hostel for visiting writers: When the store closed at night, they were free to sleep on cots or in sleeping bags among the bookshelves, and were often fed soup and wine from George's own kitchen. Over the years Whitman managed to host an estimated 50,000 people in this way, many of whom might otherwise not

George Whitman at Shakespeare & Co.

have been able to visit Paris (or perhaps would have ended up on park benches). Ginsberg, Burroughs, Orlovsky, Corso, Ferlinghetti, Norse, and others either stayed overnight or had readings at the bookshop (or both). Whitman died in his apartment above the store on December 14, 2011, at the age of ninety-eight. His daughter carries on the bookstore tradition to this day, and literary travelers are still welcomed as "tumbleweeds," invited to stay overnight in exchange for a bit of work and the promise of writerly efforts.

3. William S. Burroughs. William Burroughs spent several years in Paris, and many of his books, most notably *Naked Lunch, Minutes To Go,* and *The Exterminator,* were either written or assembled here. He made his first trip to Paris in 1933, escaping the Midwest for the summer with

William Burroughs

his friend David Kammerer from St. Louis. (This was the very same David Kammerer who would be killed ten years later by Lucien Carr in New York City, a murder that figures prominently in the history of the Beat Generation.)

In 1936 Burroughs took another trip to Paris, but it wasn't until January 1958 that he settled down to live here, leaving Tangier to take a room in the Beat Hotel. His life was in crisis at the time, and he signed up for psychological analysis with one Dr. Schlumberger. Brion Gysin arrived in Paris later that spring and bumped into Burroughs on **Place Saint-Michel**. They hadn't cared much for one another in Tangier, but now they struck up a friendship that was to last the rest of their lives. On April 13, 1958, Burroughs joined Allen Ginsberg and Gregory Corso to give a small reading at George Whitman's Mistral Bookshop: Burroughs read a section of *Naked Lunch* that had just appeared in the *Chicago Review.* Corso and Ginsberg encouraged the shy and private Burroughs to go with them to bohemian parties, where they met French artists and writers including Man Ray, Marcel Duchamp, and Henri Michaux. Before long Burroughs' addiction to heroin began to take its toll and he became more reclusive, often staying alone in his room at the Beat Hotel for days on end.

In the summer of 1959 Burroughs met Ian Sommerville, a young student working in George Whitman's bookstore, and they became lovers for a period of time. Burroughs had just been arrested in connection with a drug affair in Tangier and had decided it was time to kick his habit. In August, Sommerville moved into the Beat Hotel to help Burroughs get off drugs. The cure was torturous but successful, and the criminal charges against William resulted in only a fine and a suspended sentence. It was an important year for Burroughs in other ways as well. On October 1, 1959, while cutting a mount for a picture in his room at the Beat Hotel, Brion Gysin sliced through some newspapers and by chance invented the cut-up method. What at first seemed like only an interesting accident to Gysin became an obsession with Burroughs. For years he experimented with the process of cutting up pieces of writing and pasting them back together in random ways, trying to discover the true meanings below the surface of the words.

After a stint in England, Burroughs returned to France in 1962, in an unsuccessful effort to wrest his overdue royalties for *Naked Lunch* from Maurice Girodias, the owner of the Olympia Press. When Mme. Rachou sold the Beat Hotel in January 1963, William moved to an apartment in the Hotel Pax [**30, rue Saint-André-des-Arts**]. In the years that followed, Burroughs visited Paris frequently, even flying from Kansas in 1985 when he learned that his old friend Brion Gysin was terminally ill. In the last decades of his life his trips were more often centered around readings and public appearances.

4. Brion Gysin. William Burroughs' friend and collaborator Brion Gysin lived in Paris for many years. On his first visit to Paris in the summer of 1938 he met Jane and Paul Bowles, who would become his close friends; in fact it was Paul Bowles who encouraged Gysin to move to Tangier. Twenty years later, when Gysin left Morocco for Paris, he moved into the Beat Hotel. Here he invented the cut-up method that Burroughs found so inspiring, and along with Ian Sommerville he developed the Dreamachine, a device that used stroboscopic light to create visual hallucinations. Burroughs and others used the machine to induce visions, and incorporated some of those visions into their writings. Gysin died in his apartment at **135, rue St. Martin** in July 1986.

5. Allen Ginsberg and Peter Orlovsky. As a boy, Allen Ginsberg dreamed of visiting Paris and all the European capitals, but it wasn't until he was over thirty years old that he made his first trip. In mid-September 1957, he and his companion Peter Orlovsky arrived in Paris, hoping to stay with Gregory Corso. When Corso turned out to be unavailable—he was on an unscheduled trip to Amsterdam to hide from his creditors—they walked around all night, awed by the city's beauty. The next night they stayed near Place Pigalle, and then they moved on to Holland to find their friend on the lam. When the three of them returned to Paris together the following month, they moved into the Beat Hotel on the Rue Gît-le-Cœur, all of them sharing the same small room until Corso moved into an inexpensive attic room of his own. The Beat Hotel became Ginsberg's preferred address whenever he was in Paris.

Ginsberg and Orlovsky in their room at the Beat Hotel. 1957–58

Photo by Chapman

In Paris, Ginsberg continued to act as his friends' unofficial agent, as was his wont, lobbying Maurice Girodias to publish Burroughs' *Naked Lunch* and then helping with editorial work on the book. Allen wrote some of his best poetry on that first trip, including "To Aunt Rose," "At Apollinaire's Grave," and the very first drafts of "Kaddish," often considered his greatest work. Some of the poems were written in the hotel, but many were composed as he sat at a table in the Café Select [**99, boulevard du Montparnasse**]. The Select seems to have been Ginsberg's favorite among the many cafés he frequented, though he sometimes took Alan Ansen to a bar called the Caveau de la Huchette [**5, rue de la Huchette**] where they hoped to pick up men.

Peter sailed for America on January 17, 1958, and on the same day William Burroughs made his arrival in Paris, conveniently timed, given that he had a crush on Ginsberg and was jealous of Orlovsky. Allen remained in Paris for six more months, giving readings at venues in and around the city, and making side trips to England. Just before Ginsberg returned to America in July, he and Burroughs visited the French writer Henri Michaux, who lived on **Rue Séguier**, and whose experiences with mescaline intrigued them as much as his poetry. Years later, Ginsberg wrote an introduction to a translation of Michaux's book *By Surprise* in which he describes their various meetings and discussions during the Paris years.

On April 1, 1961, Ginsberg and Orlovsky returned to France on board the S.S. *America* and once

Photo © Allen Ginsberg LLC

Man Ray, Peter Orlovsky, and Gnsberg in Paris

Allen Ginsberg, Gregory Corso, Ed Freeman, Peter Orlovsky in Paris

again settled into a room at the Beat Hotel. (This time the envious Burroughs made it a point to leave for Tangier just before Allen's ship arrived so that he wouldn't have to see them.)

Over the course of the next thirty-five years Ginsberg returned to Paris dozens of times. In the summer of 1967 he hosted his father, the poet Louis Ginsberg, who was traveling in Europe for the first time with Allen's stepmother, Edith. As Ginsberg became more and more famous, his trips to Europe centered around readings in Paris and other cities. Sometimes these were small, intimate affairs and at other times, such as the 1982 UNESCO "War On War" festival, they included dozens of other international writers. In 1990 the FNAC Galerie mounted a giant exhibition of Ginsberg's photography and Allen was on hand for the opening. Two years later he was awarded the "Chevalier de l'Ordre des Artes et des Lettres" by Jacques Lang, the French Minister of Culture. His last trip to Paris was in 1996, less than a year before his death.

6. Gregory Corso. Gregory Corso spent a great deal of time in Paris, perhaps more time than any other Beat writer. In late 1956, he and his girlfriend Hope Savage planned a trip to Europe, but Gregory was ambivalent about leaving the U.S. Hope sailed alone for Paris, and by the time Corso arrived in March 1957, she had already left for parts unknown. At first Corso lived in a room at the Hotel des Écoles on **rue de la Sorbonne** with a woman named Nicole whom he had met by chance. He was living here when Jack Kerouac stopped to visit in April. Gregory, afraid of incurring the wrath of his landlady, wouldn't let Jack stay with him, and Kerouac left the city a few days later, blaming Corso for the rapid depletion of his cash.

Gregory Corso in his tiny attic room at the Beat Hotel

Within a few months, Corso moved in with another friend at **26, rue Saint Benoît**, where he managed to stay rent-free for a while, and then he moved on to another cheap apartment at **123, rue de Sèvres**, where he had a bed and cooking privileges. It wasn't long before he discovered the little hotel on rue Gît-le-Cœur—in fact, it was Corso who had the distinction of dubbing it "The Beat Hotel" sometime in early September 1957. While living in the Beat Hotel in 1957–58, Corso wrote many of the poems that were collected in *The Happy Birthday of Death,* including his most famous poem, "Bomb." Images of Paris creep into his poetry in lines such as "A bird looks like me | flying over the Monoprix" (a reference to a large French retail store), or "I dreamed Ted Williams | leaning at night | against the Eiffel Tower, weeping."

Once the word was out, all the poets began to stay at the Beat Hotel on their trips to Paris, until all of the rooms seemed to merge at times into one continual literary salon. Gregory preferred to write privately in his own room and then go to Ginsberg's or Burroughs' rooms for socializing. Cheap as it was, Corso could not always pay the rent, so from time to time he had to move to even more rock-bottom places like the Hotel de L'Académie [**32, rue**

Allen Ginsberg and Gregory Corso in Paris

des Saints-Pères]. But he could most often be found on rue Gît-le-Cœur, faithful to the hotel until it closed. The ever sociable Corso made many friends in Paris, including well-known artists and writers such as Jean Genet, whom he met in March of 1958. That same spring Corso introduced Burroughs to a wealthy polio victim named Jacques Stern who was interested in the Beats and drugs (not necessarily in that order). For a while, Stern became part of the Beat Hotel circle. The availability of heroin in Paris led Corso to develop his first habit. Over the course of the next forty years, drugs would take their toll on Gregory, and his creative output declined as a result.

In 1961, Corso was living with still another friend, the artist Guy Harloff, in his room at **33, Rue St. André-des-Arts**, another short-lived arrangement. He then moved on to the American Hotel [**14, rue Bréa**] and the Hotel Stella [**41, rue Monsieur le Prince**]. During the 1960s he became engrossed in the study of geometry and ancient hieroglyphics, topics that would be assimilated into his works.

By 1975 Corso was living with Jocelyn Stern in her mother's house at **67, avenue Paul Doumer**, awaiting the arrival of their baby, Max. Gregory used this address for several years, a short respite from his usual habit of serial moves; though he was still heavily involved with drugs, this was a more stable living arrangement for him than most. When his relationship with Stern came to an end, he once again lived on his own, and by 1983 he could be found in a room at **11, rue Scribe**. It would be impossible to track all the locations where Corso slept over the years, sometimes moving daily from place to place, but these will serve as examples of his peripatetic wanderings.

7. Harold Norse. Paris was the European city where Harold Norse most wanted to live. It was also beyond his means, but in May 1959 he was given the opportunity to house-sit for a wealthy friend. His host put him in a backyard studio at **9, rue Thiers**, an out-of-the-way place that he soon found boring. As he wrote in his autobiography, *Memoirs of a Bastard Angel*, "I had artistic freedom, no financial worries, and no life." Three weeks later Norse was able to move into a small, cozy apartment owned by the same friend on the **rue St. Louis en l'Île**, where he was asked to keep watch over a collection of antiques. Here he met a lover and had an affair that lasted the better part of a year. While living in the neighborhood, Norse would often

Gregory Corso and Harold Norse in front of Notre-Dame Cathedral, Paris

23

sit in the cafés, especially Les Nuages in St. Germain, and talk with friends like Gregory Corso or Jim Jones, author of *From Here To Eternity*. In late June 1959, Corso told Norse to look up William Burroughs, and the two met for the first time in the Tabac St. Michel café [**22, rue Saint-André-des-Arts**]. In addition to frequenting the cafés in the area, Norse could also be found at the Mistral Bookshop or at Gaït Frogé's Librairie Anglaise at **42, rue de Seine**, both bookstores where English-language writers were welcome. To support himself Norse taught and worked at George Whitman's bookshop. It was at the Mistral that Norse met Ian Sommerville. Knowing that Sommerville liked older men, Norse introduced Ian to Burroughs that summer.

Following his stint as a house-sitter, Norse moved to the Hôtel de l'Univers, [**6, rue Grégoire de Tours**], where he worked on cut-up poetry and pen-and-ink drawings. In March 1961, Harold Norse had his first one-man show of drawings at the nearby Librairie Anglaise. In April 1960, he ingratiated himself with Mme. Rachou at the Beat Hotel and moved in for an extended stay. Shortly after arriving he wrote the cut-up story "Sniffing Keyholes," which was to appear in his book *Beat Hotel*, though it wasn't until 1983 that an English edition of the book would be published. In *Memoirs of a Bastard Angel* he wrote, "I can't say that we attained perfect life at the Beat Hotel, but if for the artist perfect life can be defined as living in a community of fellow artists, with constant creative activity and the freedom to come and go as you please while satisfying the appetites of the flesh and to have all this in Paris when you were still young enough to subject the body to long bouts of sensual explorations and dissipations, then we lived the perfect life."

8. Lawrence Ferlinghetti

The white sun of Paris
softens sidewalks
sketches white shadows on skylights
traps a black cat
on a distant balcony

On a 1980 trip to Paris, Lawrence Ferlinghetti wrote a long series of poems called "Paris Transformations," which move back and forth across the city from the Gare du Nord to Montparnasse to Père Lachaise to Place Saint Sulpice. It wasn't the first time that the city of Paris played a central role in his writing, and it wouldn't be the last. In addition to countless poems written in and about Paris, Lawrence's two published novels, *Her* and *Love in the Days of Rage* are set in the city as well.

Ferlinghetti probably passed through Paris for the first time as a baby, on his way to his new home in eastern France with his aunt. Since he lived the first five years of his life here, French came easily to him, and following World War II he studied for his doctorate at the Sorbonne under the G.I. Bill. From January 1948 until the fall of 1949 he received a monthly government check for $65 to attend classes, and wrote and successfully defended a dissertation titled "La Cité Symbole dans la Poésie Moderne de Langue Anglaise (A la Recherche d'une Tradition Métropolitaine)." At first he lived with the Edgar Letellier family at **2, place Voltaire**, not far

Photo Courtesy of City Lights Archive

Lawrence Ferlinghetti's Student ID card photo, Sorbonne, Paris

Lawrence Ferlinghetti and George Whitman at Shakespeare & Co.

from Place Bastille, before moving to Montparnasse [**89, rue de Vaugirard**]. Here he worked on a novel called *The Way of Dispossession*. (Although he entered the manuscript in a contest run by the publisher Doubleday, Doran and Co., it was never published.)

These Paris years were formative for Ferlinghetti. It was here that he first met his lifelong friend George Whitman, whose sister Mary he had known as a student at Columbia University. At that time Whitman was selling textbooks to the American students out of a book-crammed, windowless room at the Hôtel Suez [**31, boulevard Saint-Michel**]. On their first meeting, Whitman sold Ferlinghetti a volume of Proust while sitting in a rocking chair and cooking himself dinner in a tin can over a tiny stove. The tone was set for an enduring friendship. (After Whitman opened the Mistral Bookshop in 1951 and Ferlinghetti founded City Lights Bookshop in San Francisco in 1953, they often talked about swapping stores.)

In the summer of 1948, on his way to study at the Sorbonne, Ferlinghetti met a woman named Marie Birmingham on a ship bound for France. She and her friend Mary Louise Barrett lived on **Rue du Cherche-Midi**, the same street as the fictional characters in Djuna Barnes' novel *Nightwood.* They gave him a copy of that book, and it had a great impact on Ferlinghetti's own work. Later, Marie married a French painter, Claude Ponsot, and Lawrence pub-

lished a collection of Marie Ponsot's poems as the fifth in the City Lights Pocket Poets Series (directly following Ginsberg's *Howl and Other Poems*).

The poems of René Char also influenced Ferlinghetti, and in his first book of poetry, *Pictures of the Gone World,* he writes, remembering those early days in France: "In Paris in a loud dark winter | when the sun was something in | Provence | when I came upon the poetry | of René Char | I saw Vaucluse again | in a summer of sauterelles. . . . "

Lawrence and his roommate, Ivan Cousins, often sat in cafés because there was no heat in their apartment. "Our concierge looked upon us as Communists and treated us badly," Ferlinghetti wrote. "One might call it a localized front in the Cold War." On chilly days they frequented Les Deux Magots [**6, place Saint-Germain-des-Prés**], the terrace of Le Dôme Café [**109, boulevard du Montparnasse**], and especially Le Select [**99, boulevard du Montparnasse**]. In Le Select, Ferlinghetti often saw Samuel Beckett, but was too shy to say hello. This was also the period when Ferlinghetti began to paint, an art he would continue to practice for the rest of his life. He went to drawing sessions at the Académie Julien [**31, rue du Dragon**] and the Académie de la Grande Chaumière [renamed Académie Charpentier, **14, rue de la Grande-Chaumière**] where the artists painted from the nude for no charge. Lawrence painted the walls of his apartment

Kirby and Lawrence Ferlinghetti

white and decorated them with a large mural depicting the head of a classical nude and a quotation from Edgar Allan Poe's "To Helen."

In 1949 he met his future wife, Selden Kirby-Smith, and they hung out together in Paris discussing the work of D.H. Lawrence, her special area of study. They spent time together at the Café Mabillon [**164, boulevard Saint-Germain**] and on occasion he took her to the Comédie Française [**2, rue de Richelieu**].

Although he has resided permanently in San Francisco since 1951, Ferlinghetti has always retained a special relationship with Paris, returning again and again. On a 1963 trip he stayed at the Hôtel de Seine on **Rue de Seine** and found the city changed, yet haunted by old memories: "Thus returned to Paris thirteen years later . . . still the loneliest city in the world, now buried in a welter of automobiles, traffic lights and neon. . . . Walked about the night city for about three hours. . . . Walked into the dark courtyard of 89 rue de Vaugirard, where I had my two room cave those years, pressed the minuterie, and the hall and courtyard lights came on. Saw the shuttered window of my room on the courtyard, felt the new front door.

Photo by Denise Casablanca

Jean-Jacques Lebel and Lawrence Ferlinghetti, 1965

The lights go off again." On this trip he spent time with Jean-Jacques Lebel, an anarchist painter and writer who was to translate the works of many Beat writers and become a friend to most of them. Lebel organized a reading for Lawrence and Harold Norse at the **American Centre [261, boulevard Raspail]** in Montparnasse—Lawrence and Jean-Jacques made a splash by coming onstage wearing gas masks. Two years later, in 1965, Lebel organized the International Festival of Free Expression, and Ferlinghetti again made the trip to Paris. On this trip he brought Kirby and his two children with him, and had a chance meeting with Philip Lamantia on the streets. Philip introduced Lawrence to Nancy Peters, who was traveling with him. Peters would later become Ferlinghetti's business partner and co-publisher at City Lights.

In 1968, Ferlinghetti was again in Paris, this time involved in the May student uprisings. He mimeographed activist newsletters, and witnessed the confrontation with police in **Place Maubert** during which protestors pulled paving stones from the street to use as barricades. His novel *Love in the Days of Rage* is based on this turbulent period of time. In the following years Ferlinghetti

returned more than a dozen times and wrote a good deal of poetry during his stays. *A Trip to Italy and France,* written in 1979, includes some of his best poems from that period.

In 1985 Ferlinghetti traded apartments with Jean-Jacques Lebel to pursue his art as a painter. Using a studio given to him by the Cité Internationale des Arts in the center of town, Lawrence attended more drawing sessions. In the afternoons he visited the library at the **Musée de Pompidou** where he researched the periodicals collection for background for *Love in the Days of Rage.* "Every morning I would wake up and go swimming in a pool from which you could see the Panthéon. . . . I worked out the plot of the novel while I was doing my laps. Then I would go to one or another café and write in a spiral notebook for two or three hours. Then I would go down to George Whitman's bookstore around noon or one o'clock and run into people."

9. Jack Kerouac. Though a native French speaker, Jack Kerouac visited Paris only twice: once for five days in 1957, and once in 1965 for another short stay. In April 1957, after helping Burroughs organize *Naked Lunch* in Tangier, he stopped over in Paris on his way to London, arriving at the Gare de Lyon train station hoping to enjoy a few days speaking French and seeing the sights. In *Lonesome Traveler,* Jack writes about going directly to a café on **Boulevard Diderot** to fortify himself with espresso and croissants before taking a very long walk around the city. By following Kerouac's itinerary in that book, you'll be able to see a good deal of the town. Gregory Corso wouldn't let Kerouac stay with him in his room at the Hotel Des Écoles, and Jack grumbled about having to search for his own cheap room after spending most of his money carousing with Corso that first night. While in the city, Kerouac delivered the manuscript of Burroughs' *Naked Lunch* to Bernard Frechtman, an occasional editor for the Olympia Press, who lived at **5, rue Joanès** at the time. Eventually Maurice Girodias, Olympia's owner, would agree to publish the book. During a visit to the **Louvre** Kerouac was impressed most of all by the paintings of Brueghel, David, Goya, Rembrandt, Rubens, and Tiepolo. In the days before the more con-

Photo © Allen Ginsberg LLC

Jack Kerouac posing as Gide

temporary collections were divided and sent to different museums, Van Gogh's pictures were in the Louvre, and they hit him with "an explosion of light — of bright gold and daylight."

On June 1, 1965, Jack Kerouac took his second and final trip to Paris, flying into Orly airport on an Air France jet from Florida. He had grown increasingly interested in his family's French roots and hoped that he could trace his ancestors back to their original village in Brittany, but the trip turned into a drunken fiasco, all honestly described in his short book *Satori in Paris*. He found a cheap room near Les Invalides (the burial place of Napoleon) [**129, rue de Grenelle**]. Initially he planned to look up specific rare volumes in the Bibliothèque Mazarine [**23, quai de Conti**], but the librarian informed him that the Nazis had burned the ones he needed in 1944. At the Bibliothèque Nationale [**58, rue de Richelieu**] and the Archives Nationales [**60, rue des Francs-Bourgeois**], the librarians offered little

help when they saw how drunk and disheveled he was. When he stopped at the offices of his French publisher, La Librairie Gallimard [**15, boulevard Raspail**], the secretary told the inebriated visitor claiming to be Kerouac that all the editors were out.

Other than hanging out in what he called "the perfect bar," La Gentilhommière [**14, place Saint-André-des-Arts**], near his hotel in the St. Germain district, the only thing Jack managed to do was to attend a concert of Mozart's *Requiem Mass* at the church of Saint-Germain-des-Prés [**3, place Saint-Germain-des-Prés**] with a teenage girl he had just met. One evening while sitting with his cap in his hand in the chapel of St. Louis De France [**19 bis, rue Saint Louis en l'Île**], he received the *coup de grâce*: "a woman with kids and husband comes by and lays twenty centimes (4 cents) in my poor tortured mis-understood hat (which I was holding upside-down in awe)." She had mistaken Jack for a beggar.

10. Carl Solomon. The man whom Allen Ginsberg met in a mental hospital and to whom his poem "Howl" is dedicated, Carl Solomon, was also the person who introduced Allen to a wide range of contemporary French authors. In the summer of 1947, two years before he met Ginsberg, Solomon had sailed to France with the National Maritime Union and then jumped ship. His goal was to go to Paris in search of the Surrealists and Existentialists he admired. Remembering the trip as a turning point in his life, he often talked about stopping into a gallery in St.-Germain-des-Prés on a corner of **Rue Jacob** where Antonin Artaud was, in Solomon's words, "screaming" his poetry. This whetted his taste for Artaud, whose work he studied and used as inspiration. (Artaud himself died of an over-dose the following year in Rodez.) During his six weeks in Paris, Solomon also attended a perfor-mance of *Les Bonnes (The Maids)*, Jean Genet's first play, at the Théâtre de l'Athénée [**7, rue Boudreau**], and visited the Galerie Maeght [**42, rue du Bac**] where André Breton

had disrupted an appearance by the Dadaist Tristan Tzara. In 1948 Solomon returned to Paris once again, hoping to learn more about the French literature that fascinated him. This time he attended a lecture on Kafka given by Jean-Paul Sartre at Le Palais d'Iéna [**9, place d'Iéna**] and discovered the work of Jacques Prévert.

11. Maurice Girodias. The Olympia Press was created by Maurice Girodias, a native-born Parisian whose father had founded the Obelisk Press in 1929. French law al-lowed pornographic books in English to be published and sold in France, and by marketing to foreign tourists, both father and son ran successful businesses. As the publisher of what came to be called db's (dirty books), Maurice of-ten recruited legitimate writers who needed ready cash to write these potboilers as quickly as possible. To avoid le-gal difficulties, he occasionally published "serious" litera-ture, and in that vein became famous for being the first to publish *Lolita* and *The Ginger Man*. In 1957 Jack Kerouac gave a copy of the manuscript of Burroughs' *Naked Lunch* to Bernard Frechtman, one of Girodias' editors. For two years they debated whether or not to publish the odd book, but it wasn't until Mason Hoffenberg (the co-author of *Candy*) read it and proclaimed it the "greatest greatest book" that Girodias decided to publish it. By that time the Olympia Press had offices at **7, rue Séverin**. In 1959, the

first 5,000 copies of *Naked Lunch* sold quickly, but Girodias was notorious for not paying his authors. Futile attempts to obtain royalties from this stingy, nearly bankrupt publisher would become a fixture of Burroughs' life.

In 1961 the Olympia Press published Gregory Corso's first and only novel, *The American Express.* It didn't sell well, and Gregory did not have to worry about collecting royalties. By that time Maurice was heavily in debt due to his investments in his chic restaurant La Grande Séverine, which operated on the ground floor of the same building as the publishing company— on April 24, Gregory was given a publication party here. In December 1961 Girodias also began to publish *Olympia Magazine,* which featured work by many Beat writers including Ginsberg, Burroughs, Corso, Gysin, Alex Trocchi, and others.

12. Others. Nearly every writer of the Beat Generation has made at least one trip to Paris during their lives. Robert Creeley and his family stopped in Paris for a few days in 1951 en route to their new home in Fontrousse, but Creeley was sick in bed, which made their stay a disappointing one. A high point was a visit to the Paul Fachetti Gallery [**6, rue des Saints-Pères**], where Creeley saw an exhibition of paintings by Jackson Pollock that made a tremendous impression on him. He and Charles Olson compared what Pollock was doing in painting to what they would like to do in poetry, breaking away from the purely pictorial.

After being married in Jerusalem, Janine Pommy Vega and her husband Fernando moved to Paris, where Janine sold copies of the *New York Times* on the street and worked as a folksinger to scrape together a meager living.

Occasionally she also posed for art classes at L'École des Beaux-Arts [**14, rue Bonaparte**]. They moved from one cheap hotel to another until they found an inexpensive apartment near the Porte Saint-Denis in the tenth arrondissement. In November 1965, Fernando died of a heroin overdose in Ibiza while Janine was in Paris trying to sell one of his paintings. The tragedy left Janine stranded in France until her parents sent her money to get back to New York.

The poet John Giorno became a close friend of Brion Gysin and William Burroughs while they were all living in Paris during the 1960s. Giorno often combined his love of Pop Art with his interest in poetry to create cut-up and montage texts. Brion Gysin helped him apply those techniques to audio recordings, and his first audio poem cut-up was played at the 1965 Paris Museum of Modern Art Biennale.

Ted Joans also lived in Paris on and off for many years. When he was not in Africa or America he could be found at Shakespeare & Co. or along the Boulevard Saint-Germain-des-Prés in one of his favorite cafés. When he read his poetry at La Pensée Sauvage, a bookstore on **Rue l'Odéon**, people laughed at his witty poem "I Will Sell Paris." Before his death, Joans stayed at **40, rue de la Montagne**.

FRANCE

MEUDON

1. Louis-Ferdinand Céline. In early July 1958, Allen Ginsberg and William S. Burroughs visited the French novelist Louis-Ferdinand Céline in the Parisian suburb of Meudon. Céline lived in a house surrounded by an overgrown garden filled with rusting junk at **25, route des Gardes**. Ginsberg and Burroughs were eager to meet the great novelist, whose work they had known and respected since the early forties: Allen cited Melville, Céline, Genet, and Dostoyevsky as major influences on them. The older Céline told Burroughs, who shared his love of black humor in the observation of horrible events, that the way to get to "know a country [is] thru its jails"—advice Burroughs thought was true to his own experience. When Céline died suddenly due to an aneurism in 1961, he was buried in Meudon's Cimetière de Longs-Réages [**26, Rue Marais**].

NORMANDY

1. Lawrence Ferlinghetti. On June 6, 1944, Lawrence Ferlinghetti, along with nearly 73,000 other Americans,

took part in the largest amphibious invasion in history. As a U.S. naval officer he commanded a subchaser off the coast of Normandy during the D-Day invasion. His ship was used as a screening vessel, and thus he didn't land on the beach; their mission was successful, since no U-boat attacks occurred that day. After the worst of the battle was over, they tied up to a breakwater made of sunken Liberty Ships just offshore, but the boat's propeller became tangled in the floating debris and threatened to sink them. The ship was saved through the quick action of Ferlinghetti and his crew, and they managed to

Photo Courtesy of City Lights Archive

Lawrence Ferlinghetti at Normandy, 1944

limp back to Plymouth, England, on one engine.

On VE Day—May 8, 1945—Lawrence was stationed in nearby Cherbourg. He and his junior officer decided to take a jeep and drive to Paris, but the jeep broke down and they ended up in the small port town of Saint Brieuc on the south side of the Cherbourg Peninsula. As Ferlinghetti tells the story, "There was this café full of people on Liberation Day. Everyone was getting drunk and singing, and I saw the little line of Prévert, a little verse of his on the tablecloth. These poems were passed around during the French Underground. That's why it was called *Paroles*, it not only meant 'words,' it meant 'passwords.'"

Ferlinghetti would later begin to translate Prévert's poems while in Paris on the G.I. Bill, and once in San Francisco he translated more of them until he had enough for a book. In 1958 he published those poems as *Paroles*, Number Nine in the City Lights Pocket Poets Series.

MORLAIX

1. Lawrence Ferlinghetti. During a long trip to Europe in the early eighties, Lawrence Ferlinghetti found himself sitting in the Café de la Terrasse [**7, rue Duplessis de Grenedan**] in Morlaix, a small town on the coast of Brittany. The setting inspired him to pen a poem on the spot. He titled it "Morlaix: Into the Future with Neil Young" and included it in his collection *Over All the Obscene Boundaries*. In this poem he mentions the Morlaix viaduct that

arches above the town; although it resembles an ancient Roman aqueduct it is actually a mid-nineteenth-century railroad bridge. Lawrence captures a fleeting sense of time and place in the poem by describing an old horse that walks into the Place de la Mairie.

> An old nag clops around a corner
> into the Place de la Mairie
> Suddenly following the horse
> an amazing cavalcade appears
> a troupe of masked mummers
> to the sound of a flute and a small tambour
> beaten with a stick

BREST

1. Jack Kerouac. On Kerouac's April 1965 visit to France, after he gave up hope of finding documentation in Parisian libraries about his ancestors, Jack decided to fly to Brest, hoping for better luck tracing his lineage in Brittany itself. When he got drunk and missed his plane, he took a train instead, arriving at the Brest railroad station late at night. At that point no one would rent him a room, so he wandered alone through the streets of town. Fearing that he might be mugged in his drunken condition, he went to the local police precinct, where they took pity on him and kindly found a room for him in a little Breton inn on **Rue Victor Hugo**. The next day someone suggested he look up Pierre "Ulysse" Lebris, an old man who ran a nearby restaurant, which Jack did. Lebris was one of the old Kerouac family names, but Jack's branch of the family had left Brittany hundreds of years earlier and there was no way to confirm his relationship with anyone still living. Discouraged with his entire trip, Kerouac left Brest that same day for Paris and then immediately flew back to his mother's home in Florida.

Since Kerouac's death, other family members have continued to research Kerouac genealogy and found that some of Jack's ancestors came from the town of Huelgoat, a few miles east of Brest. One of these ancestors, Urbain-François Le Bihan de Kervoac, fled to Quebec in the 1720s to avoid prison––the exact missing link between France and the New World that Jack had been searching for.

CHARLEVILLE

1. Allen Ginsberg. On his December 1982 European tour, Allen Ginsberg was invited to attend a conference on the French poet Arthur Rimbaud (1854–91) in the poet's hometown of Charleville. As a bonus, Allen was able to spend two nights in Rimbaud's own apartment, where the poet had lived as a teen from 1869 to 1875. When Ginsberg was there in 1982 it served as a guest house; the building has since been converted into a museum called "Maison des Illustres" [**7, quai Rimbaud**] on the banks of the Meuse River. Allen spent his spare time during his stay writing dozens of postcards to friends in America. To Robert Creeley he described a late-night apparition: "I've been staying in the apartment where he [Rimbaud] wrote *Lettres du Voyant* and *Bateau Ivre*. Woke 4 AM to pee in Rimbaud's old toilet, saw a strange shadow by the door." Hoping that he was experiencing a brush with the illustrious ghost of Rimbaud, Allen was disappointed to realize that "it was the T.V. set!"

STRASBOURG

1. Lawrence Ferlinghetti. A few months before Lawrence Ferlinghetti's birth in Yonkers in 1919, his father died in the great influenza epidemic. Shortly after the baby was born, his mother, Clemence Mendes-Monsanto, suffered a breakdown and was institutionalized. As a result

Lawrence Ferlinghetti, 1939

Photo Courtesy of City Lights Archive

Lawrence was adopted by his mother's aunt and uncle, Emily and Ludwig Mendes-Monsanto. The couple was in the midst of marital difficulties, and before long Emily left her husband and went to live in her native France, taking baby Lawrence with her. They ended up somewhere near the Alsatian capital of Strasbourg, possibly in the town of **Mulhouse**, where Emily might have had relatives or a job. Ferlinghetti's earliest memory is of being held in his "French mother's arms" on a balcony as a parade passed by. Lawrence spoke French before learning English and as a young boy considered himself to be French. In 1924 Emily reunited with Ludwig and returned to America with Lawrence. In his poem "The Photo of Emily," based on the only photograph that he had of himself with his Aunt Emily, Lawrence writes:

> She thought of herself as a writer
> as having something special to say
> in French
> I thought of her as my French mother
> . . .
> My French mother Emily stands on the bridge
> in the old photo
> the only photo I had of her
>
> . . . .
> So silent the old picture —
> If it could only speak!
> . . . .
> And saw her never again
> And never saw her again

except in the back of old boutiques
peered into now again
with haunting glance
in the Rue de Seine

AIX-EN-PROVENCE

1. Jack Kerouac. In April 1957 Jack Kerouac decided to hitchhike from Marseilles to Paris. To make his way through the urban sprawl of Marseilles, he took a bus as far as Aix-en-Provence. In *Lonesome Traveler,* he comments on the sidewalk café where he stopped to have a few glasses of vermouth. While sitting here he passed the time by observing "Cézanne's trees and the gay French Sunday" afternoon. He visited the Cathédrale Saint Sauveur [**34, Place des Martyrs-de-la-Résistance**] and wept when the young choir boys sang old hymns. The sixth-century Merovingian baptistery that he describes is still here, as is the beautiful countryside that inspired Paul Cézanne. When Kerouac left town he continued via public transportation and never did walk across France as he had originally planned.

2. Allen Ginsberg. In 1961, Allen Ginsberg and Peter Orlovsky visited Aix-en-Provence in order to absorb the beautiful view of Mont Sainte-Victoire, which figures prominently in the work of Paul Cézanne. Allen had studied Cézanne's landscapes as a student at Columbia University and was highly influenced by the way the painter seemed to transmit the substance of his own mind through his work. In a journal entry Allen wrote that he used "Cézanne's method of elimination to get a feeling of the infinite" in his early sonnets. When he finally reached Aix himself, Ginsberg bought a postcard reproduction of one of Cézanne's landscapes and wanted to compare each brushstroke in the painting with the actual site. Unfortunately, a new housing project had been built on the exact spot from which Cézanne had painted the steep south face of the mountain.

3. Kenneth Rexroth. Kenneth Rexroth, the San Francisco Renaissance poet who was an early (but always contentious) friend of the Beat writers, married his third wife Marthe Larsen in Aix-en-Provence in 1949. The newlyweds drank grog in the Deux Garçons [**53, cours Mirabeau**], a café which still serves spirits today. Both Ginsberg and Kerouac were aware of Rexroth's long poem "Aix-en-Provence." In it, Rexroth also made reference to the region's most famous artist. "Cézanne's pines are steely gray. | Mont Sainte Victoire is not blue | Or lavender in the sky, | It is pure bright limestone gray."

Kenneth Rexroth

FONTROUSSE

1. Robert Creeley. Robert and Ann Creeley and their son Dave lived in the small town of Fontrousse near Aix-en-Provence from July 1951 until January 1952. When Creeley first arrived, he found everything about the area delightful: the town, not much more than two rows of stucco houses and a small roadside chapel; the view of Mont Sainte-Victoire, painted so often by Paul Cézanne, in the distance; and the vineyard-covered hills all around.

Their two-room, two-floor house was a steal at $5 a month. Creeley became disenchanted quickly when he failed to learn French easily and began to feel isolated. To combat this feeling of solitude he began work on an autobiographical novel that was never finished. He

Robert Creeley, 1963

also wrote many poems, including "The Riddle" and "The Innocence."

> Looking to the sea, it is a line
> of unbroken mountains.
>
> It is the sky.
> It is the ground. There
> we live, on it.

LAMBESC

1. Robert Creeley. After becoming disappointed with their home in Fontrousse, Robert Creeley and his family found a larger house in nearby Lambesc. Here they enjoyed all the luxuries they hadn't had in Fontrousse, electricity foremost. Ann was pregnant and due to deliver in July 1952, which had necessitated their move. After they settled in, their child, Charlotte, was born on July 27. Creeley was able to write more here, and his poem "After Lorca" was dedicated to his new neighbor in Lambesc, M. Marti. Life was pleasant for a while, and on one afternoon Creeley even had the chance to meet Pablo Picasso. During this same period he became friendly with Martin Seymour-Smith, who lived on the island of Majorca, and because of this friendship Creeley decided to move his family there.

MARSEILLES

1. Brion Gysin. On December 21, 1958, Brion Gysin traveled to an artist's colony at **La Ciotat**, a town about twenty minutes east of Marseilles. As his bus passed through an avenue of overhanging trees, he closed his eyes against the flickering of the sunlight. "An overwhelming flood of intensely bright patterns in supernatural colors exploded behind my eyelids: a multidimensional kaleidoscope whirling out through space. The vision stopped abruptly when we left the trees," Gysin recorded in his journal. The attempt to replicate the effect eventually led Gysin and Ian Sommerville to invent the psychedelic contraption they called the "Dreamachine." The Beat Hotel in Paris may have been the Dreamachine's birthplace, but this road near Marseilles has the honor of being its place of conception.

2. Others. Marseilles was often used as a transit hub by the Beats when they traveled through Europe and Northern Africa. Jack Kerouac, Allen Ginsberg, William

Jacques Stern, Gregory Corso, Peter Orlovsky, unknown, and Allen Ginsberg in Cannes, 1961

S. Burroughs, Gregory Corso, and many other writers passed through, whether they were going to and from Tangier by ferry, or traveling across France to the Mediterranean coast. Many of them took advantage of their layover to sample the cheap narcotics and inexpensive prostitutes that could be found in the Noailles, at the time Marseilles' Arab quarter.

CANNES

1. Allen Ginsberg, Peter Orlovsky, Gregory Corso.

In late April 1961, at the invitation of Shirley Clarke, the director of the film *The Connection,* Allen Ginsberg, Peter Orlovsky, Gregory Corso, and jazz saxophonist Alan Eager took a train from Paris to the Riviera. Clarke's film (based on Jack Gelber's play of the same name) was being shown at the Cannes Film Festival. The poets stayed in a house with Clarke and the cast members, many of whom had plenty of real-life experience to help them convincingly portray addicts on film. Allen reported in a letter to Kerouac, "*The Connection* movie had a little house there outside of Cannes and so offered us the basement to inhabit free and as we were broke and without prospects we decided to hide out there and see free movies – so for a month, packets of heroin arriving from Paris by mail, the scene in the villa same as on movie screen." In his journal Peter Orlovsky described the house as having a beautiful setting about six kilometers from the film festival. "Right out my window a pineapple tree with a hundred long curved arms to look at and imagine I'm on an island far away from America and also a hill curve in the near distance topped by a long row of trees," he wrote. On the days when they took a bus into Cannes they spent most of their time sitting in the Blue Bar [**42, boulevard Croisette**] near the main theater of the film festival.

NICE

1. Gregory Corso. The early poems of Gregory Corso often revolve around a single concept or noun such as "marriage," "power," or "army." In Nice in May of 1957, after disastrous financial losses at the casino in Monte Carlo, he found himself literally starving. He had lost all his money and didn't know anyone in the south of France who could support him. After five days without a meal, little wonder that he would find himself writing the poem "Food," which appeared in his collection *The Happy Birthday of Death.*

> Hunger! petty agent of Death,
> If anything to mature me, *you!*
> Five-day sister making paper of me.
> Sadder than the Last Supper
> I eat nothing
> — Melancholy learns to starve.

While deciding on his next move, the starving Corso went to an opening of a Joan Miró exhibition at the Galerie Matarasso [**2, rue Longchamp**]. Here he met Pablo Picasso and Josep Llorens Artigas. Gregory managed to confuse them all by arguing about what was meant by brown: "Not the color," he shouted. No one (including Gregory) knew what he was talking about. Writing to Ferlinghetti, Corso described the incident: "He [Picasso] and Artigas walked away. The gallery

Gregory Corso

Photo by Gui de Angulo

owner was bugged by me. I wore no tie – my pants were dirty and I had crashed the opening. I walked out screaming: 'Goodbye! Goodbye!' Picasso's eyes bulged. Artigas bowed. Miró smiled faintly. Thus a day in Nice." Artigas and Miró took pity on him and treated him to lunch the following day, and thus his fast was broken.

SPAIN

BARCELONA

1. Gregory Corso. In May 1957, Gregory Corso left Paris and took a short trip through France and Spain, stopping in Barcelona for a few days. For no apparent reason, he purchased a gun, which he would subsequently take back to Paris. (Eventually, while drunk, he threatened to commit suicide with it in front of a Paris café, necessitating its quick disposal once the police arrived.) While on his Barcelona trip Corso wrote to Ginsberg, "Barcelona is filled with cheap shoes and beautiful whores and sad bulls—you'll like Barcelona—Lots of English and Germans and Spaniards here."

2. Allen Ginsberg. In June 1957, Allen Ginsberg and Peter Orlovsky arrived in Barcelona on their way to Italy. Allen was reminded of his father's 1937 poem "When Bombs on Barcelona Burst," written during the Spanish Civil War. Allen and Peter walked up **La Rambla**, the huge street made for walking and shopping that cuts through the center of the city. They enjoyed eight-peseta meals in "dark downstairs Rembrandtesque workingman's restaurants," and rented a hotel room that they imagined must be reminiscent of a Paris garret. They went out but "couldn't find any wild Genet life—so went to ancient old stained glass cathedrals, vast pillars and caves, and a museum Meyer Schapiro'd have dug, best collection Romanesque painting in world." Having settled for architecture instead of depravity, they found that the "wildest" monument in Barcelona was the unfinished **La Sagrada Familia [Carrer de Mallorca, 401]** designed by architect Antoni Gaudí, "so weirdly balanced it scares you way up inside especially as it's already cracking and huge windows held together only by lately acquired rusty pieces of wire and whole balconies crumbling with jagged cracks in soft stone."

MADRID

1. Lawrence Ferlinghetti. In 1950, on his way to Majorca, Lawrence Ferlinghetti stopped in Madrid, where he was captivated by the city's art museums. He wanted to see the paintings at the Prado in particular, but was surprised that the one artist who inspired him more than the others was Joaquín Sorolla y Bastida, a painter from Valencia whose home is now a museum devoted to his work [Museo Sorolla, **Paseo del General Martinez Campos, 37**]. In his poem about the paintings, Ferlinghetti wrote (misspelling his name):

> Sarolla's women in their picture hats
> stretched upon his canvas beaches
> beguiled the Spanish Impressionists
> And were they fraudulent pictures
> of the world
> the way the light played on them
> creating illusions
> of love?

Ferlinghetti returned to Madrid in the summer of 1963. This time he was particularly moved by the grotesque visions of Hieronymus Bosch at the Prado, writing: "'El Bosco'—his world one huge Gothic hell, a medieval inferno of people & creatures *doing things to each other* (so too Wm. Burroughs 'unlocked his word hoard'). The world of the Bosco Kid: a woman being eaten by a blue insect with hairy beak as blackbirds fly out of her asshole. . . ." After describing more details of the paintings at length, Ferlinghetti concluded, "One thing about Bosch's people I never

Lawrence Ferlinghetti

understood: Why none of them have erections. . . ." He also noticed the statue of Goya at the side entrance to the Prado, which he mentions in his poem "Goya & the Sleep of Reason":

> The dark stone statue of Goya
> stands between the trees
> at the side entrance of
> the Museo del Prado
> He wears a long greatcoat
> and carries a tall beaver hat
> Larger than life he
> strides forward purposely
> on a pedestal on top of
> a four-sided bas-relief
> carved in white stone
> in which are depicted
> various struggling figures
> from his outrageous collection
> of humans and inhumans

2. Allen Ginsberg and Peter Orlovsky. In June 1957, Allen Ginsberg and Peter Orlovsky visited Madrid on their first European trip. Allen, who loved museums and could never get enough of them, spent his time visiting the Prado while Peter recuperated in the hotel room from a case of food poisoning. Like Ferlinghetti, Ginsberg was impressed with the Bosch paintings that he found here, but he particularly loved one of the masterpieces of the Prado's collection, "La Anunciación" by Fra Angelico. Ginsberg was less delighted by the bullfight he attended: he sympathized with the plight of the bull. When he returned to Madrid almost forty years later in 1993 he no longer needed to find the cheapest hotel in town and stayed at the elegant Hotel Suecia [**Calle del Marqués de Casa Riera, 4**].

3. William S. Burroughs. Unlike the other Beat writers, William Burroughs was not particularly enchanted with Madrid, as he seemed to find nothing but trouble. After visiting the Prado for a mere half hour and spending the rest of his brief sojourn lying in bed with a "mystery illness," he crossed Madrid off his list of places to live. In

Kiki and William S. Burroughs on the Socco Chico in Tangier

1967 he lost the contract for *Junky* when his bags went missing at the airport in Madrid. It was also in Madrid that his Spanish companion Kiki had been murdered in 1957. Burroughs and Kiki had lived together in Tangier, but Kiki took off for Madrid with a Cuban singer, and when the Cuban caught Kiki in bed with a woman he stabbed him with a kitchen knife.

NERJA

1. Lawrence Ferlinghetti. In 1965 Lawrence Ferlinghetti and his family spent three months in the coastal fishing village of Nerja, in Andalucía. In February they rented a small house at **Calle Carabeo, 72**, which he described as a "tiny house. White walls, tile floors, dirt street full of big rocks and broken cobbles, on cliffs over the beach." The house proved to be too cold and drafty for them, and three weeks later they moved to a larger house on the same street [**Calle Carabeo, 68**], where they remained until May. The newer house had "six big bedrooms, a big dining room and kitchen, a single bathroom with cold water, a sink in the kitchen made of a piece of marble, a big long empty studio upstairs and a tile veranda downstairs opening onto a vegetable & fruit garden." While living in Nerja, Ferlinghetti discovered the poetry of Pablo Picasso, which led to City Lights' 1968 publication of a selection of his poems, translated by Paul Blackburn under the title *Hunk of Skin: Pocket Poets Series Number 25*. Ferlinghetti also took an interest in the politics of Spain under the repressive regime of Francisco Franco. The long poem he composed on the subject, "The Free Spirit Turning Thru Spain," grew to twenty pages but was left unfinished. When Ferlinghetti

was not writing or reading, he took the family on short side trips to the nearby towns of Granada, Málaga, and Seville. In Seville he stopped in at the Antigua Taberna de Las Escobas [**Calle Álvarez Quintero, 62**], where both Alexandre Dumas and Lord Byron had once dined, and witnessed a spontaneous, wine-fueled battle of flamenco guitar and *cante jondo* singers. Closer to home, the family also explored the recently discovered Caves of Nerja, which stretch for several miles beneath the hills. Ferlinghetti lamented the demise of the town when he saw the construction of a new resort hotel, "looking like a harmonica . . . on the cliffs above the biggest beach, with a colony of Miami-type duplex houses rising up behind it." He presciently predicted that it was "probably the last year for Nerja and its old way of life." Still, his visit there inspired him to write several poems, including "Telegram From Spain" and "Into Darkness, In Granada."

2. Philip Lamantia and Nancy Peters. In 1963, Lamantia was living in Rome when his ex-wife, Goldian, invited him to join her and her husband, André Vandenbroeck, who were living at **Calle Carabeo, 72** in the village of Nerja. When Philip arrived in February, he

Nancy Joyce Peters

rented a tiny white-washed stone house near his friends at **Calle Carabeo, 68**. By curious coincidence, these were the very same two houses that Lawrence Ferlinghetti would rent in 1965, without having any idea that Lamantia had lived here two years earlier. Philip had given up poetry (for good, he thought) and he welcomed Goldian and André's invitation to study

Egyptian geometry, architecture, and iconography, subjects of deep interest to them all. By July, however, the three had gone their separate ways, Philip to Tangier, and the Vandenbroecks to the Aurobindo ashram in Pondicherry, India.

In 1966 Philip moved back to Nerja with his wife, Nancy Peters, who would become an editor at City Lights in 1971. They rented the same house at Calle Carabeo, 68 for $20 a month, living a simple life without central heat, television, refrigerator, or car. (And in their turn, they had no idea that Lawrence Ferlinghetti had lived

Philip Lamantia

in the house the year before.) Life in Nerja was filled with writing, reading, new friends, immersion in gypsy Flamenco music, and visits to Gerald Brenan in the nearby town of Alhaurín el Grande. (Brenan, a member of the Bloomsbury Group and the author of several books on Spanish literature and history, had left Spain when the war began but was permitted to return in 1953 in spite of his anti-Franco views.) Many of the poems in Lamantia's *The Blood of the Air* were written in Nerja.

MAJORCA

1. Lawrence Ferlinghetti. After receiving his doctorate from the Sorbonne, Lawrence Ferlinghetti spent the summer of 1950 in the small fishing village of Puerto de Andraitx, near Palma on the island of Majorca, where he rented a house on the beach with a few friends. Initially Ferlinghetti's plans for that summer had been to travel around the Mediterranean and visit the Greek isles, but he never got farther than Majorca. While living here he worked on a manuscript of a long series of poems called "Palimpsest," which remains unpublished today. It contains many allusions to the sea and the fishermen he observed along the coast.

While Lawrence was on Majorca, he was paid a visit by Selden Kirby-Smith, whom he had been seeing in Paris. She came for a week, bringing her mother along as a chaperone and staying in a nearby pension. Kirby hoped that Lawrence would propose to her, and shortly after she left he sent her a telegram saying, "Will you marry me?" Proving to be a reluctant groom, he changed his mind several times in the following months, but on April 10, 1951 they were married in Florida, and eventually settled permanently in San Francisco.

2. Robert Creeley. After living in southern France, Robert Creeley moved to Majorca in the summer of 1952. He found life here peaceful enough, but didn't particularly like Robert Graves, who at the time was the island's main literary lion. Graves was "really one hell of a bore," Creeley wrote to poet Irving Layton. The Creeleys found a spacious and inexpensive house to rent in Bañalbufar, a town on the north side of the island, about 15 miles from Palma. During his stay on Majorca, Creeley published Paul Blackburn's *Proensa* under the imprint of the Roebuck Press; he also founded the Divers Press and worked on the first issue of *Black Mountain Review*. By March 1954, what had at first seemed like paradise to Creeley began to sour, and he headed off to teach at Black Mountain College in North Carolina, leaving his family behind. He returned to Majorca when the school year was over and became friends with Edward Dahlberg. In 1960–63, Creeley fictionalized his experiences of this period in his novel *The Island*.

MONACO

MONTE CARLO

1. Gregory Corso. None of the Beat writers appear to have been gamblers, with the exception of Gregory Corso. In the rare times when he had money, he was more than willing to wager it all (and usually lose it) at the gaming tables. In November 1958, Corso took the money he had received from the sale of his earliest manuscripts to Monte Carlo and managed to lose $300 in a short period of time. While in the casino he met the author James Jones—who had made a good deal of money in 1953 when his novel *From Here to Eternity* was turned into a popular movie— and they struck up a short friendship. In a letter about the meeting, Gregory wrote, "We had a mad talk about criminals and he said that only the criminal mind could exist in the world today, but that they shouldn't brag that they're criminals. Jazz musicians, he said, are making it because they're criminals and are cool about it. I would have none of that so I jumped up with laughter and joy and said: 'No, no, I brag to you I am a criminal, a criminal!' At that very moment about five Monte Carlo unnoticeable guards became noticeably alert." Gregory claimed to be the highest bidder at the dice table that night. "I bet the limit. I always thought Monte Carlo was so splendidly extravagant and mad and fortune suicide world, but no, just a lot of silly people hung on money, that's all. No color. No pretty sophisticated ladies, no nothing." A "real draggy place," he concluded.

Chris MacLaine, Peter Orlovsky, and Gregory Corso

ITALY

MILAN

1. Nanda Pivano. The most important link between the Beat Generation and Italian readers was Fernanda Pivano, who lived in Milan for much of her life. Over the years, Nanda, as she was known, wrote and edited countless books about the Beat Generation. She also translated nearly all of the important Beat writers, including Kerouac, Burroughs, Ginsberg, Ferlinghetti, and Corso. Her versions of Beat Generation literature became the basic texts in Italy. Early in her career, Nanda was the first to translate Edgar Lee Masters' *Spoon River Anthology* into Italian, and it soon became one of the most important American books in Italy. Then in 1948 she met Ernest Hemingway and translated his *A Farewell to Arms,* thereby becoming known as a major proponent of American literature all over Italy. Later, as she grew to be a friend and translator of most of the Beat writers, she often hosted them on their trips to Milan. Her books *Viaggi Cose Persone* and *The Beat Goes On* document her life with the Beats, and include many rare photographs. In 1958, when the Beats began traveling to Italy, she was living with her husband, the well-known Olivetti designer Ettore Sottsass, in an apart-

Photo © Allen Ginsberg LLC

Nanda Pivano and her husband Ettore Sottsass

ment at **19 Via Cappuccio**. In 1967 they moved to **14 Via Manzoni,** and in 1983 they moved once more to an apartment at **13 Via Senato,** where Pivano ended up living by herself after they broke up.

Pivano acted as Jack Kerouac's translator and host when he flew to Milan in September 1966 to promote Mondadori's publication of *Big Sur.* Allen Ginsberg and Peter Orlovsky never failed to visit Nanda during their Italian trips, and it was Pivano who arranged the first meeting between Ginsberg and Ezra Pound. She died in Milan on August 18, 2009.

2. Gregory Corso. In the spring of 1960, Gregory Corso made his first trip to Milan. Here Nanda Pivano introduced him to the Italian poet and Nobel Prize winner Salvatore Quasimodo. Corso wrote that he "found him great! and after that read him, and found his poesy greater!" In 1965 Corso returned to Milan to stay at **69 Corso Magenta** with a friend, Leo Lionni. While he was living here he tried to produce a literary magazine for the publisher Feltrinelli with submissions from all his friends, but the project fell through.

3. Allen Ginsberg. While traveling in Milan in 1967 Allen Ginsberg penned his antiwar poem "Pentagon Exorcism." Although he couldn't be with the protestors in Washington who were planning to levitate the Pentagon, he felt that his poem might help serve the cause from afar. Ginsberg returned to Milan again and again, as recently as June 1995, for readings and visits with his translator, Nanda Pivano.

4. Lawrence Ferlinghetti. From time to timeLawrence Ferlinghetti also visited the city and took inspiration from it. In his 1980s poem "Ristorante Vittoria, Milan," taking his usual feeling of alienation amongst the upper class

Lawrence Ferlinghetti in Brescia, 2002

to absurd lengths, he wrote about overhearing three men at the next table discussing deep-sea mining in accented English: "I decide to pretend I don't understand | the strange language they are talking [. . .] putting my meat in my mouth | with the fork in the left hand | in the Continental manner | having read an international spy novel | in which the American fugitive | gives himself away | by changing his fork back to his right hand. . . . " He was also sitting in a Milanese hotel when he received the telephone call that inspired his poem, "How Clear Your Voice From Belgrade."

BRESCIA

1. Lawrence Ferlinghetti. Carlo Leopoldo Ferlinghetti, Lawrence Ferlinghetti's father, was born in the town of Brescia about 1872. He emigrated to the United States in the 1890s and settled in New York with his wife Clemence, shortening the family name to Ferling in the process. In 2005 Ferlinghetti returned to Brescia, searching for his family roots. He discovered the address of his father's birthplace, **Contrada da Cossere 20**, but when he knocked on the door of the house the owner took him for a burglar (evidently a very polite one) and called the police. The misunderstanding made the headlines of national papers all over Italy. Let the incident be a warning to users of this guidebook!

While in Brescia, Ferlinghetti was inspired by the cobbled piazza in the center of town to convert a section of San Francisco's Vallejo Street in North Beach, between the Caffè Trieste and the Church of St. Francis, into a similar open plaza. It would be called the Piazza Saint Francis (or alternatively, The Poets' Plaza). Lawrence and a group of collaborators have shepherded the project through its municipal planning stages since then, but as of this writing the project has yet to be realized.

VENICE

1. Alan Ansen. In the fall of 1954, after Alan Ansen had gone on a tour of European cities, he decided to settle in Venice. He would remain here for the next four or five years before relocating to Athens for the rest of his life. Venice appears in several of his poems.

> Tamed by an income, by beauty and the water,
> Hemmed in by palaces lighter than air,
> By churches that bring a city square to order
> And tactfully arrange a scene, a life

Alan Ansen in front of St. Mark's, Venice

While in Venice, Ansen stood out as an expatriate, made even more visible by the bright red suit he often wore. He hosted many of the Beats and introduced them to his Venice friends, people like Peggy Guggenheim, Willem de Kooning, and James Merrill. In the summer of 1956, William

Burroughs came to Venice to stay with Ansen. Burroughs wasn't particularly interested in the art and architecture of the city, but he did like to go out on the lagoon to practice his rowing skills, one of the few forms of exercise he enjoyed. At the time Ansen was living in the top-floor apartment at **3219 Calle Carrozze**, near San Samuele. By the summer of 1957, when Allen Ginsberg and Peter Orlovsky first arrived in Venice for a visit, Ansen had settled in and knew the city well. He took them to the Jewish ghetto and Allen photographed him here with the local street urchins. Ansen was mortified when Ginsberg and Orlovsky argued at a dinner given for Peggy Guggenheim and began tossing a wet towel back and forth across the table. This social gaffe got Allen and Peter blackballed from Guggenheim's company, but Ansen was invited back. Everyone was far more amused, though, when Orlovsky dove into the Grand Canal fully clothed one afternoon. In 1959 Ansen composed his first of many masques, *The Return From Greece*, to celebrate Peggy Guggenheim's sixty-first birthday. It was performed for her at her palazzo, which is now the Peggy Guggenheim Collection **Dorsoduro, 701**.

William Burroughs rowing in the lagoon, Venice, 1956

2. Gregory Corso. Gregory Corso was another of the frequent visitors who stayed with Ansen during his time in Venice. In those days Alan's small monthly trust fund check was enough to pay the rent and have a little left over to share with friends. Corso was always willing to take advantage of Alan's hospitality when he got into financial difficulties elsewhere in Europe, and he spent a good deal of time during the late fifties in Venice. He and Ansen collaborated on some poems, including "Heroin: An Ode," which Ansen eventually rewrote and published. In 1958 Corso had a brief affair with the wealthy art collector Peggy Guggenheim. As he reported gleefully to Ron Loewinsohn, "Yesterday had mad wild time with Peggy Guggenheim in her huge mad house dancing in and out the Picassos and D'Chiricos and the Arps and what not, she wore butterfly spectacles and streamlined witchy shoes, and I wore nakedness and a Zebra sheet, she is a great woman, and Venice has become seemingly romantic as she has become a sort of George Sand for me." A longer involvement was not to be, since before long Corso made some rude comments about Peggy's daughter, Pegeen, and the romance ended abruptly.

Gregory Corso and Alan Ansen in front of St. Mark's, Venice

3. Allen Ginsberg. In the fall of 1967 Allen Ginsberg went to Venice for the sole purpose of visiting the American poet Ezra Pound, with the permission of Pound's companion, Olga Rudge. He stayed for several weeks, walking over to Pound's house at **252 Calle**

Allen Ginsberg in front of St. Mark's, Venice, 1957

Querini each day. Pound remained almost completely silent during these visits, even though Ginsberg talked to him continually and played contemporary records for him in an attempt to prove that the Beatles and Bob Dylan were true poets. Ginsberg did manage to coax a scant few words out of Pound each time, and that was enough to keep him happy. He was invited to the house on Pound's eighty-second birthday, and this became a high point of Allen's European journeys.

In 1995 Ginsberg was back in Venice again, this time for the opening of an exhibition of his photography displayed at the Venice Biennial. He shared space with a new friend, the Japanese artist Hiro Yamagata.

RAPALLO

1. Ezra Pound and Allen Ginsberg. Allen Ginsberg was fascinated by Ezra Pound. As early as 1953 he had tried to visit Pound at St. Elizabeth's Mental Hospital in Washington, DC, where the elder poet was being detained due to his pro-Fascist work during World War II. Ginsberg asked their common friend William Carlos

Ezra Pound, Allen Ginsberg, and Nanda Pivano, 1967

Williams for an introduction, but Pound's response was to tell Williams to "keep his nuts to himself." Through the efforts of Ginsberg's Italian translator, Nanda Pivano, Pound finally agreed to see Ginsberg for coffee in the fall of 1967. Ginsberg and Pivano drove to a small town near Rapallo and met Pound and his companion, Olga Rudge, for a quiet afternoon in a café. This broke the ground for Rudge to permit Ginsberg to visit Pound in Venice.

FLORENCE

1. Gregory Corso. In 1958 Gregory Corso made his first trip to Florence, a place he described to Ginsberg as a "city of beautiful bodies and music of stone." He would return again and again. On his second visit in 1960 he sat on a hill in nearby Fiesole, overlooking Florence, and wrote the poem "Saint Francis," his homage to the great frescoes of the life of St. Francis by the painter Giotto. It begins: "I praise you your love, | Your benediction of animals and men, | When the night-horn blew, | And the world's property was disproportioned." Later in his life he met the singer Patti Smith on one trip to Florence and the two walked through the renaissance streets late into the night talking about history, art, and poetry.

2. Lawrence Ferlinghetti. On several occasions Lawrence Ferlinghetti also visited the historic town. In 1980 he noted his impressions of the trip into town, "Driving into Florence from the West | From the freeway through | the flashing cars and new | high room apartments | and glass houses | to the old city | by the old Arno | with its old bridges. . . . " For a while a group of younger admirers ran a bookstore and publishing company in Florence which they called City Lights Italia (or Luci della Città) [**Via di San Niccolò 23**]. Although it was never a part of Ferlinghetti's San Francisco business, Lawrence gave them his blessing. They hosted many readings and invited Beat writers such as Anne Waldman and Ed Sanders to perform here.

In July 1986, the World Congress of Poets was staged in Florence and attracted many people, including both Corso and Ferlinghetti.

Photo by Roberto Cavallini

Lawrence Ferlinghetti and Marco Cassini of City Lights Italia, 1996

PISA

1. Lawrence Ferlinghetti. Probably everyone instantly recognizes Italy's most famous tourist site, the leaning tower in Pisa. Each Beat writer passing through the area made a point to see it as well. In his poem "Canti Toscani" Lawrence Ferlinghetti writes:

> Tower of Pisa
> leans away from the sun
> which turns dark red
> as its day's work
> is done
> and then falls down
> on the red tile roofs
> and pulls them down
> and pulls down the town
> into darkness
> Only the tower stands up
> as night fills
> my cup

Ferlinghetti went one step further and when he got back to San Francisco suggested that the city fathers consider tilting the Coit Tower on Telegraph Hill. "Think what it did for Pisa," he said.

ASSISI

1. Allen Ginsberg and Peter Orlovsky. In August 1957, Allen Ginsberg and Peter Orlovsky took a train from Rome to Assisi and spent two days exploring the area. Ginsberg had read several biographies of St. Francis and was touched by his teachings. They visited the **Porziuncola**, St. Francis' small chapel where he began the Franciscan brotherhood in 1208, and they hiked up to visit the **Hermitage** where the famous saint communed with nature. At night they slept in the grass in front of the monastery in Assisi. Unfortunately, they weren't welcomed with open arms when the priests of the monastery discovered them camped out on the front lawn, and an argument ensued. Allen wrote, "I got the impression they'd be bugged by St. Francis himself if he reappeared on the streets of Assisi in his tattered cloak begging and singing in the streets like he used to."

SPOLETO

1. Festival of the Two Worlds. When Gian Carlo Menotti founded the Festival of the Two Worlds in 1958 in the small town of Spoleto, no one would have believed that it would grow to become one of the world's premier art extravaganzas. The festival began as a series

of musical programs, but at some point Menotti began to invite poets too. In June 1965, Lawrence Ferlinghetti was invited to read, and this gave him a chance to meet Ezra Pound, who was also scheduled to appear. The experience inspired a prose poem that Lawrence titled "Pound At Spoleto." In it, Ferlinghetti describes seeing the older poet in the setting of the lovely Teatro Melisso [**Piazza del Duomo, 1**], "still as a mandarin statue in a box in a balcony at the back of the theatre." The presence of Pound greatly moved Ferlinghetti: "The voice knocked me down, so soft,

Photo by Ettore Sottsass

Police talking to Allen Ginsberg after his arrest at the Festival of the Two Worlds, Spoleto, 1967

so thin, so frail, so stubborn still. I put my head on my arms on the velvet sill of the box. I was surprised to see a single tear drop on my knee." Yevgeny Yevtushenko read his poetry at Spoleto that same year, even though there were rumors that he wouldn't attend in protest against Pound who was still considered to be a Fascist by many.

In 1966 it was Gregory Corso's turn to read at the festival, and the following year, 1967, Allen Ginsberg was asked to read. Just as Ferlinghetti had, Ginsberg got to meet his literary hero Pound at the festival. Ginsberg's own reading was somewhat more dramatic: he was arrested by the police for using what they considered to be obscene language. It took years to have the case thrown out by the Italian judiciary, but it made great press for the festival.

ROME

1. Gregory Corso. Rome was central in the life of Gregory Corso. He first saw the eternal city in 1958 and fell in love immediately, spending many subsequent years hanging out in its streets and piazzas. It was in Rome that he began to use the history of Western civilization as a component in his poetry, and from then on his work drew inspiration from mythology, archaeology, and the classics. In a 1958 letter to Gary Snyder, Corso wrote: "I wonder if there can be anything more lovelier than Rome or Greek in ruins? It's those Roman inscriptions thin and worn, those half-columns, those missing noses – nothing except perhaps, Egyptian ruins can come close – The colossess, the foro, Nero's palace – The past is true – it is not a lie, it has not been made up – It's all here! Shelley – Caesar, Augustus, Vespasius, Keats, Michelangelo, the new Pope, Giovanni XXIII!!"

Corso's nomadic lifestyle makes it difficult to ascribe

particular apartments to him. Often he used friends' addresses as mail drops and may or may not have actually been living there. He usually stayed in cheap hotels or lived with friends, acquaintances, and even strangers whenever he could. He proved to be a difficult house guest and often wore out his welcome and was asked to leave. During the 1960s he stayed with Patrick Creagh and his family at **3 Piazza Campo**. Creagh had met Corso in 1966 while organizing the poetry readings for Spoleto's Festival of the Two Worlds. In the mid-1980s, Corso used the address of a friend named Rutilo at **30 Via Capo D'Africa**, near the Colosseum. Later in that decade he stayed with Francis Kuipers at **21 Via Natale del Grande** in Trastevere.

During the day Corso hung out mainly in places close to his drug connections, feeding the habit he had picked up in Paris. At the time, the **Campo de' Fiori** was a center of illicit drug deals, and it therefore became one of his favorite haunts. While waiting to score, he would often sit at a table at the Vineria Reggio [**15 Campo de' Fiori**]. He loved to explain the significance of the statue of Giordano Bruno that looms over the square. Bruno was a monk burned at the stake by the Roman Inquisition for his beliefs, someone whose persecution Gregory probably identified with.

And of course Corso visited the ancient ruins and studied their stories. In his poem "On Palatine" he describes the view looking down onto the Roman Forum.

> Via Sacra I look down upon you,
> my ownself tribunal,
> before six-columned Saturnus
> and tri-graced Castor and Pollux

So strong was Gregory's love for the Romantic poet Percy Bysshe Shelley that, after his death in Minnesota in 2001, Corso's family and friends arranged for his ashes to be interred in a plot at the feet of Shelley in the Cimitero Acattolico, commonly called the Protestant Cemetery [**6 Via Caio Cestio**]. On Corso's tombstone this poem is inscribed:

Gregory Corso's grave, Rome

> Spirit
> is Life
> It flows thru
> the death of me
> endlessly
> like a river
> unafraid
> of becoming
> the sea

2. Allen Ginsberg. Even before Corso paid his respects, Allen Ginsberg visited the graves of Shelley and Keats. On his very first day in Rome, August 2, 1957, Ginsberg walked out to the cemetery to pay his respects to the great poets and plucked a clover leaf from Shelley's grave. "Kissed Shelley's grave goodbye," he wrote, and then continued on a four-day whirlwind self-guided tour of Rome. Always a tireless tourist, Ginsberg, along with his companion Peter Orlovsky, visited the Colosseum, the Forum, the Pantheon, St. Peter's, the Vatican Museums, and dozens of other spots before moving on to the town of Assisi. On this first trip to Rome, Allen became livid when he saw that earlier popes had placed fig leaves over the genitals of the nude statues. "I almost flipped there, it is maddening after all the beautiful nakedness of David in Florence," he wrote. Exercising his keen eye, he wrote a poem, "Forum, Rome" describing a fragment of a frieze he discovered:

Look at all these broken stones,
and by the wall
The rainstained fragment of an ass
a human ass
was here two thousand years ago
— some boy turned round
stuck out his behind
and posed
Michelangelo remembered
when the palaces had fallen —
When the cities are forgotten
there'll be a human ass

Ginsberg visited the city dozens of times, performing and giving readings and lectures at numerous venues. On one memorable visit to Europe in 1967, Allen invited his poet father, Louis Ginsberg, and stepmother Edith to accompany him. In Rome Allen splurged on rooms for them at the Hotel d'Inghilterra [**14 Via Bocca di Leone**], a luxury hotel well beyond his usual means. One night Allen slipped out to cruise the nearby Spanish Steps. While he was talking to the long-haired hippies and flirting with the young boys, the police conducted one of their periodic raids, sweeping Allen up with the rest. Allen had to call his father to come to the police station and identify him, and Louis was understanding enough to share a good laugh with him over it.

Allen Ginsberg in Rome, 1957

Photo © Allen Ginsberg LLC

3. Harold Norse. When he first went to Rome in 1953, Harold Norse found a cheap room in the back of a decaying palazzo on the **Via dei Serpenti** where he stayed for a few months. He returned in 1957 and found work teaching English for the next two years at the Lion School of English on the **Via del Babuino**. At that time he moved into a nicer apartment in the row of red brick houses along the **Via dei Foraggi**, nestled quietly beneath the ruins on the Palatine Hill. While in Rome he too cruised the Spanish Steps and wrote a great deal of poetry. He also set to work translating some of the 2,000 sonnets of the Roman poet Giuseppe Belli, famous for his use of an inner-city Roman dialect, which reminded Norse of his own Brooklyn speech pattern. One of Norse's own poems, "Victor Emmanuel Monument," attracted the unwanted attention of the government when he mentioned that the guards were often available as sexual partners, "picking up extra cash from man and boy." Italian officials were incensed, and the poem created a minor scandal, nearly causing Norse to be deported. In his *Memoirs of a Bastard Angel* Harold writes about his friendships with Alberto Moravia, Elsa Morante, and Pier Paolo Pasolini, whom he often met for coffee at Rosati's [**5A Piazza del Popolo**], a café that still bustles with Romans and tourists alike.

4. Jack Kerouac. Once in 1966 Jack Kerouac visited Rome on a publicity tour hosted by his Italian publisher, Mondadori. He didn't have to give any readings, but he was scheduled for interviews and press conferences promoting the new Italian translation of *Big Sur,* the 500th book in Mondadori's distinguished *La Medusa* series. Kerouac met people for coffee at Rosati's and dined next door at the elegant restaurant Dal Bolognese [**Piazza del Popolo ½**], where he made rude comments about the chic Cinecittà clientele. By this time in his life he was drinking heavily and had lost all interest in sightseeing and adventure. Jack preferred to be left alone in his room at the Albergo Barberini [**3 Via Rasella**], but as he was a devout Catholic, we can assume that he appreciated the visit to Vatican City arranged for him by his hosts.

It was in Taddei's, a bar on the **Via del Babuino**, that Kerouac met Franco Angeli, an Italian artist. One afternoon Jack went to Angeli's studio at **41 Via Oslavia** and collaborated with him on a painting of the crucifixion. The painting was lost and never heard of again until 2011, when the canvas was discovered and exhibited in a retrospective of Angeli's work in a gallery at the Victor Emmanuel Monument.

5. John Clellon Holmes. Shortly after Kerouac's trip, John Clellon Holmes and his wife, Shirley, stopped in Rome as part of Holmes's own European tour. Holmes was hoping to sell articles to a travel magazine, but he never found a publisher. By 1966 he had also succumbed to alcoholism and was depressed from traveling. Eager to get home, he wasn't much impressed by Rome. All he saw was a city of ruins; everything around him seemed to be decaying with age. Walking in the **Pincio Gardens** near the

Villa Borghese, through the paths lined with countless busts of celebrated Italians, he noted their weathered, stained faces. On the parapet overlooking a fabulous panorama of the city in front of the Villa Medici [**1 Viale Trinita dei Monti**] he spotted the aging movie star Tab Hunter leaning against the wall. The ruins around the **Largo Argentina** had been

John Clellon Holmes

abandoned to feral cats, and he wrote that even the posh cafés along the **Via Veneto** featured in Fellini's *La Dolce Vita* held no particular interest for him. Holmes, like many other Beat writers, noted his visit to the room in which John Keats died of tuberculosis in 1821 [**26 Piazza di Spagna**]. Then he stopped for yet another drink at the Caffè Greco [**86 Via Condotti**] along with a horde of other tourists. Disillusioned, the couple left Rome after only a few days, heading for Naples, the last stop on their tour.

6. William S. Burroughs and Alan Ansen. Perhaps William Burroughs was singular in his dislike of Italy. He sailed to Rome in December 1953 and moved in with Alan Ansen, who had only just arrived himself. Burroughs wrote to Ginsberg, "As for Rome, in all my experience as a traveler I never see a more miserable place. I would rather be in Bogotá, yes even in Quito." (See the Latin America section of this book for the full import of this statement.) For Ansen's part, he wrote to Ginsberg disputing this negative response, saying, "The fountains are wonderful (even old Cactus Boy melted at the sight of Trevi), and I feel that in spite of minor irritations Europe is just wonderful." Ansen's attempt to rent an apartment in Rome fell through because the landlord took a dislike to the prickly Burroughs, and on January 4, 1954, William left for Tangier. Before long Ansen moved on to Florence, Munich, Paris, London, and finally Venice, where he settled down to live for a number of years.

Alan Ansen in front of St. Peter's in Rome, 1954

7. Others. As fame touched the Beat writers, they traveled more and more for readings and conferences. Nearly everyone was invited to Rome at least once, even those who generally preferred Zen and the Far East over Catholicism and Western civilization. Philip Whalen was invited and made his first trip to Europe in the early 1980s. "I really dug Rome," he said, "because I was hung up on it when I was a kid, and studied Latin." In September 2004, Gary Snyder came to Rome for the publication of the Italian edition of *Turtle Island* by Stampa Alternativa. He held a press conference and reading in the city before making publicity stops in Umbria and Tuscany. (Snyder reserved the final days of his tour for himself, so that he could head north to Bolzano and visit the Archaeological Museum to see the remains of Ötzi, the so-called "Iceman" whose body had been locked in an alpine glacier for nearly 6,000 years.)

After Joanne Kyger married Jack Boyce in 1966, they took a trip to Europe, stopping in Rome. It inspired her to write "Poems from Rome," which appeared in her col-

Judith Malina, Julian Beck, and Allen Ginsberg, 1985

lection *Places to Go,* published by Black Sparrow Press. Although most of the poems aren't specifically tied to place, some site-specific inspiration is evident in poems like "Hesitation", which begins with, "I wouldn't put it together any other way. | The walls were torn down from Hadrian's Villa. What form | is the shape we proceed in. . . . "

The Living Theatre troupe of actors led by Julian Beck and Judith Malina frequently performed in and around Rome. In 1978 the entire cast was detained by the police after their third performance of *Prometheus* at the Teatro Argentina [**Largo di Torre Argentina, 52**]. It was a harassment tactic, with arbitrary identification checks made on the actors to see if anyone was wanted anywhere on criminal charges; those hopes were disappointed and everyone was subsequently released.

OSTIA

1. Primo Festivale Internazionale dei Poeti. Perhaps the most famous reading abroad to involve Beat writers took place on the beach at Castelporziano near Ostia in June 1979. Ferlinghetti, Ginsberg, Corso, Orlovsky, di Prima, Hirschman, and Nanda Pivano were all invited for a three-day event that the promoters billed as the Woodstock of poetry. It attracted 20,000 people. At one point, when the Russian poet Yevgeny Yevtushenko got up to read, anarchists in the audience made a commotion and wouldn't let him speak. A riot was averted when Allen Ginsberg and Peter Orlovsky took control of the microphone and managed to calm the audience. Later the crowd did allow Yevtushenko to read without further disturbance.

The festival took place on the same beach where Italian poet Pier

Paolo Pasolini had been murdered a few years earlier, in 1975. In his "Canti Romani," Ferlinghetti writes:

> the dust of one *ragazzo di vita*
> who fell here
> where we stand
> with reporters and *paparazzi*
> wanting to know what we think
> of the murder here
> of one Pier Paolo Pasolini

As a matter of fact, Ferlinghetti hadn't actually read Pasolini at the time of the festival, so he had to fly by the seat of his pants when the reporters asked him questions about what he thought of the Italian poet. After this attention-catching introduction, Lawrence began to read and translate Pasolini. In 2001 his translations were published by City Lights Books as *Roman Poems*.

ANZIO

1. Sebastian Sampas. In January 1944, Jack Kerouac's closest childhood friend, Sebastian "Sammy" Sampas, took part in the U.S. Army's storming of the beaches of Anzio. It was one of the worst battles of the Second World War, and Sampas was severely wounded. He died of those wounds on March 2, 1944. His death made a lasting impression on the young Kerouac, and Sampas appears in several of his books. Twenty years later, Jack would marry Sammy's sister, Stella.

NAPLES

1. Harold Norse. Naples was the home of Virgil, Alessandro Scarlatti, and Nero, but Harold Norse was the only one of the Beat writers to live there for any length of time. He spent a busy year here in 1958–59, teaching, writing poetry, and pursuing romantic interests. Norse was employed by the USIS as an English teacher and taught classes at the American Studies Center on the third floor of the palazzo they once leased in the **Largo Ferrantina a Chiaia**. At that time Norse rented an apartment at Grottomare [**38**

Entrance to Harold Norse's house in Naples, Italy

Via Posillipo] and had what might have been the most spectacular view that any Beat writer ever enjoyed: a panorama of the city, a view of the bay, and Mount Vesuvius were all visible from his perch on the side of a cliff. One of his best poems from the period, "Classic Frieze in a Garage," records a walk from this apartment to his teaching job, passing the umber-colored embassies along the Marghellina waterfront. Here, amidst the "oil and greasy rags" of an auto repair garage, he spotted an incongruous ancient fresco: "I saw Hermes in the rainbow of the dark oil on the floor."

His poem "Piccolo Paradiso" tells of a short-lived romance he had that year. To his lover he writes, "remember this | the wine | the ladder | the stars that climb | Vesuvius outside | my window | the waves | banging into smooth | tufa cave."

2. Allen Ginsberg. While on his way to visit W. H. Auden on Ischia, Allen Ginsberg, like so many other visitors, stopped to explore nearby Pompeii. As he described the trip, "Climbed up Vesuvius and spent an hour looking at steam coming out of the rocks in the walls of the great crater on top; and then slid and walked down the side thru pulverized lava sand and down lava fields into beautiful grape growing country (picking and eating delicious blue grapes along the road) and down further to the Bay of Naples and the ruins of Pompeii. Spent the end of the afternoon walking thru those deserted and strange streets. Still quite a bit of statuary and painting left there including a lot of naked Venuses and satyrs and drunken Bacchuses, mythological figures all over the walls, including a set of priapic illustrations in a ruined ancient bordello." Before leaving the area he spent an afternoon at the "ruins of Cuma where Cumaean Sibyl had caves and prophecies,"

One discovery Allen reported to all of his friends was the "secret cabinet" of pornographic sculpture and mosaics at the Museo Archeologico Nazionale di Napoli [**19 Piazza Museo**]. In those days you had to ask the guard to unlock the door, but nowadays the collection is open to all visitors, although a disclaimer warns that some more prudish than Ginsberg may find the exhibit offensive.

In 1967 Ginsberg returned to Naples and visited the famous Italian poet Salvatore Quasimodo, who would die there the following year. On a 1981 trip, Ginsberg read at the San Carlo Opera House [**Piazza del Plebiscito**] with Amiri Baraka. They filled the 1,300 seats of the royal theater built in 1737, one of the oldest in Europe. Fernanda Pivano came along to act as translator.

3. Amiri Baraka [LeRoi Jones].

Amiri Baraka

After reading with Ginsberg at the Opera House in 1981, Amiri Baraka returned to Naples in 2005 at the invitation of the Casa della Poesia to read with Jack Hirschman at the **Teatro del Parco dei Camaldoli**, an amphitheater in the hills above the city. Amiri created a furor when he read "Somebody Blew Up America," his poem about the 9/11 terrorist attack on the World Trade Center. In the poem Baraka suggests that the Israelis knew of the plot well in advance and had considered it an opportunity to create hostility between America and the Islamic world.

4. Jack Kerouac. On his 1967 book tour Jack Kerouac spent a few days in Naples and managed to create a scene wherever he went. At a press conference held at the Villa Pignatelli [**201 Via Principessa Rosina Pignatelli**] he defended the U.S. military role in Vietnam. His right-wing opinion shocked the liberal students from the university, who had expected "the King of the Beatniks" to be antiwar like Ginsberg. The audience began shouting and "I snuck out like a football player," Jack wrote, "and ran to our sports car. Zoom!" While Jack was in town his publisher Mondadori put him up in the posh Hotel Royal, now the Hotel Royal Continental [**38/44 Via Partenope**], overlooking the sea. He was also interviewed in the large lecture room on the second floor of the renowned Libreria Guida [**20/23 Via Port'Alba**]. The owner of that bookstore, Mario Guida, still remembers escorting Jack around town. He said it was his job "to carry the beer." One evening a tipsy Kerouac climbed onto the stage at the Otto Jazz Club [**23 Salita Cariati**] and stumbled through a few old Frank Sinatra tunes in front of the audience.

5. John Clellon Holmes. Coincidentally, John Clellon Holmes made Naples the final stop of his 1967 tour of Europe in December, just a few months after Kerouac's visit. Holmes and his wife arrived by train at the new Stazione Termini [**Corso Giuseppe Garibaldi**], tired and depressed after four months on the road. They checked into the Hotel Rex [**12 Via Palepoli**] expecting the worst, but the visit proved to be cathartic for Holmes, and it renewed his enthusiasm for life. Although he described the city as "festooned with loaded wash lines, littered with stale vegetable greens, ill-lit, pestilential, a filthy rabbit-warren of steep alleys raw with onion, and tenements as noisome and noisy with the stench and uproar by which the poor insulate themselves," he found that there was "a feeling of *neighborhood,* of a community created out of passions, appetites, and dangers suffered in common." He titled the essay he wrote about his visit "See Naples and Live," playing on the familiar quotation, "See Naples and Die" (perhaps first penned by Virgil).

6. Others. The Living Theatre performed numerous times in Naples, and their work has been staged at the Teatro San Ferdinando, the Teatro Politeama, the Teatro Mediterraneo, and many other venues around town. Their first Neapolitan production was "The Brig," which they produced in May 1965. In 2003 a giant retrospective exhibition called "The Living Theatre: Labirinti dell'Immaginario" was mounted in the Castel Sant'Elmo, one of the city's most beautiful and famous museums. The coffee-table-size exhibition catalogue is indispensable to any scholar of the Living Theatre.

Like so many others, Gregory Corso was intrigued by the antiquities of classical Greece and Rome that he

found everywhere in Naples. Early on he discovered the Sybil's caves at Cuma and returned there several times, as did writer Kaye McDonough, the mother of Gregory's youngest child, Nile. In later years Gregory spent a few weeks in nearby Positano at the home of his friend, the Australian artist Vali Myers.

Lawrence Ferlinghetti stopped in Naples on several Italian trips. On one of his more recent visits he recalls having lunch with the city's mayor in a café on the Piazza Dante. They had orecchiette (ear-shaped pasta) and the mayor joked that Neapolitans who heard too much had to eat their ears, referencing the pervasive presence of organized crime in daily life. Lawrence thought it a witty commentary.

ISCHIA

1. W.H. Auden. The poet W.H. Auden made the town of **Forio** on the island of Ischia his summer home every year from 1948 to 1957, entertaining visitors including Tennessee Williams and Truman Capote. Several of the Beats were also associated with him: Alan Ansen, who had been Auden's secretary during the 1940s in New York City, visited him on Ischia, as did Allen Ginsberg, who had lived in Auden's same Lower East Side neighborhood in Manhattan. In 1957, Ginsberg made a pilgrimage to visit Auden while in southern Italy, taking a ferry from Naples. He found Auden in Marie's, his favorite café on the **Piazza Matteotti**, which is still in the center of Forio, a tiny town on the west coast of the island. Ginsberg did not feel welcomed when Auden told him that he didn't see anything to revolt against and that he didn't like Walt Whitman or Allen's politics. The two poets argued, and Ginsberg left with the impression that Auden was just a cranky old man.

Over the years Auden stayed in many different places, including the Pensione Nettuno [**1 Via Cesare Piro**] and the albergo Di Lustro [**9 Via Erasmo Di Lustro**]. The year after Ginsberg's visit, when Auden was unable to buy a house on Ischia, he began to vacation at Kirchstetten in Austria instead, and never returned to the island.

AMALFI

1. Allen Ginsberg. In June 1995, Allen Ginsberg flew to Naples and took a car to the vacation home of the artists Francesco and Alba Clemente in Amalfi. The poet was beginning to suffer from a severe illness that would take his life two years later, and the Clementes had offered him a week of rest in their villa. Ginsberg, always unable to relax completely, wrote dozens of letters to his friends telling them that he was resting. On a postcard to his stepmother, Edith, he wrote, "Food fresh, pasta local, lemon trees in backyard garden and terraces behind roomy apartment newly tiled – I have bedroom & bath to myself – 180 steps up into crowded jumble of houses up the hill from beach, hotels, shops, tourists, sea food restaurants where we eat lunch while [watching 2 year] old twins bathe. Arches top of hill across from me is graveyard, red tile roofs below – I sleep late, sun deck has big view of Mediterranean, great place to convalesce & rest a whole week, nothing to do."

Francesco Clemente

Photo © Allen Ginsberg LLC

CEFALÙ, SICILY

1. Living Theatre. In the winter and spring of 1968, the Living Theatre found a comfortable refuge at the Club Méditerranée [**Club Med, Galleria S. Lucia**] in the little town of Cefalù, east of Palermo. Here they worked on one of their greatest productions, "Paradise Now," parts of which they later performed in the streets of the town. Eventually the scandal created by the anarchist play led to problems everywhere it was performed. After its premiere at the Avignon Festival that summer, it was banned by Avignon's mayor. Julian Beck, Judith Malina, and the rest of the Living Theatre troupe continued performing the play undeterred across Europe and America, everywhere meeting with resistance from police and politicians alike.

GREECE

ATHENS

1. Gregory Corso. Of all the Beat poets who had an interest in the classical world, no one was more captivated by Greece than Gregory Corso. His first trip to Athens was in September 1959, and he commemorated it with a poem called "First Night on the Acropolis" which appears in his collection *Long Live Man*: "And the moon like a woman's breast | Nippled the Parthenon full," he wrote, evidently smitten. This poem was followed by others such as "Greece," "Reflection in a Green Arena," and "Some Greek Writings," all grounded in the ancient sites he loved. He spent months at a time in Athens, enough time to pick a fight with a *Life* photographer, witness President Eisenhower's motorcade pass by on a state visit, and have a drink with boxing champion Primo Carnera.

In letters back to his friends Corso wrote that he was "filled with Athens and know well its tower of winds Acropolis Agora stoas etc." He studied the history of classical Greece at every opportunity and drank far too much ouzo in the local tavernas. He didn't need the ouzo, though, to find everything magical, from the gymnasium of Diogenes to the caryatids of the Erechtheion.

In January 1961 he wrote inviting Ginsberg and

Orlovsky to visit. "I have a three room apartment right underneath the Acropolis. And only a few feet away, on both sides, from the Roman Agora, and Diogenes gymnasium." He remained here until April 1961, soaking in the beauty of the city and nearby ancient sites from the Peloponnese to Delphi. Corso was frequently drawn back to Greece, where he could live affordably amid the ruins. He even tried to settle here for good, spending most of 1966 in Greece trying to find a place that he could call home, but by then his addiction to drugs was beginning to undermine his poetic (and house-hunting) efforts.

2. Alan Ansen. One major reason that Corso and so many other Beat writers came to Athens was Alan Ansen, who settled here permanently in the 1960s. Ansen, the

Gregory Corso in front of the Caryatid Porch on the Acropolis, Athens

model for Rollo Greb in *On the Road* and AJ in *Naked Lunch*, was a generous and hospitable friend, and he welcomed their visits just as he had in Venice. His knowledge of the language and the city was unparalleled and he was always ready to engage in detailed literary discussions. When he first saw Athens he fell in love with the city and its liberal attitude towards homosexuality. Here he wrote much of the poetry published in his collection *Contact Highs*, was commissioned to write and stage plays, and lectured at the Athens Centre [**48 Archimidous**]. In the course of four decades he had several apartments. One on **Alopekis Street** has since been torn down, but he most recently lived at **26 Timoleontos**

Philimonos, Marasleion. His apartments were always filled with thousands of books stored on industrial metal book shelves, but near the end of his life, only his beloved Agatha Christie novels seemed to hold his interest. On November 12, 2006, Ansen passed away in an Athens nursing home at the age of eighty-three, watched over by good friends.

3. William S. Burroughs. The first time that William Burroughs visited Athens was in the summer of 1937. He was fresh out of Harvard and had met a Jewish woman, Ilse Herzfeld Klapper, who needed his help to escape the Nazis. They came to Athens to be married at the U.S. consulate, so that Ilse might be able to emigrate to the United States. The civil ceremony was performed and Ilse received the transit papers, which probably saved her life. (Ten years later, once she was established in New York, they divorced.)

In later years, Burroughs returned from time to time to visit his friend Alan Ansen, but he never settled in Athens himself. One trip took place in August 1973, when Burroughs flew to Athens to pick up some old manuscripts from Ansen, and stayed at the Hilton Hotel.

Allen Ginsberg in front of the Parthenon, Athens, 1961

Memories of this trip made their way into his 1981 novel, *Cities of the Red Night.*

4. Allen Ginsberg. Allen Ginsberg also dropped in to see Ansen every few years. In 1961, even before Ansen had settled here permanently, Ginsberg was playing the role of tourist in Greece and visited Athens, Delphi, Mt. Parnassus, Olympia, Hydra, and Crete. While sitting in a café at the Piraeus seaport, Ginsberg watched the Greek boys dancing for the tourists and was inspired to write the poem "Seabattle of Salamis Took Place Off Perama":

> Hail Jukebox of Perama with attendant minstrel juvenile whores
> on illuminated porches where kids leap to noise bouncing over black oceantide,
> leaning into azure neon with sexy steps, delicious idiot smile and young teeth, flowers in ears . . .

Ginsberg's final trip to Athens was in December 1993, when he read his poetry downtown at the Rex Theater [**48 Panepistimiou**], easily filling the 600-seat auditorium. As always, his old friend Ansen was sitting in the audience as his guest.

5. Harold Norse and Irving Rosenthal. When the Beat Hotel in Paris closed in 1963, Harold Norse left for Greece, where he divided his time for three years between Athens and various islands. In America he always feared that he would be jailed for being gay, but in Greece he found the live-and-let-live atmosphere perfect. He absorbed the ancient classical art, and countless images of Greece found their way into his poetry.

Around 1964, the editor of *Big Table* magazine, Irving Rosenthal, arrived in Athens armed with a letter of introduction from the photographer Ira Cohen. He presented it to Harold Norse, who was living in the **Plaka** just below the Acropolis at the time. Norse guided Irving around town and gave him essential advice: don't pick up boys at Papaspyros or Constitution Square; Omonia Square was much better and safer. Rosenthal was looking for a quiet place where he could finish work on his novel *Sheeper*. Norse suggested that he stay at

Harold Norse in Athens, 1964

the Kronos Hotel [**56 Panepistimiou**], where the poet Charles Henri Ford was living, but Rosenthal found it too expensive. Then, since Norse was off to the island of Hydra for the summer, he offered him the use of his own apartment. When Rosenthal warned Norse that he wouldn't allow him back into his own apartment while Rosenthal was working, Norse withdrew the offer. Irving moved into the Kronos after all, and the misunderstanding ended their friendship.

6. Philip Lamantia and Nancy Peters. In early 1965, Philip Lamantia lived at the same Kronos Hotel that Harold Norse recommended to Irving Rosenthal, just across the street from the Church of the Apostle Philip in Monastiraki, not far from the market. The hotel was the residence of a number of free-spirited expats, including Philip's old surrealist friend Charles Henri Ford. Harold Norse (the great Kronos connector) had also recommended this hotel to Nancy Peters, who arrived in Athens after traveling through the Middle East and Egypt. It was

Philip Lamantia, Nancy Joyce Peters, and Ted Joans

at the Kronos that Philip and Nancy—who would later marry—first met.

HYDRA AND THE GREEK ISLANDS

1. Gregory Corso. While he was living in Greece, Gregory Corso explored the island of **Hydra**. The first time, in 1959, while walking around an isolated area on the less-developed side of the island, he experienced a vision that would have a profound effect upon him. He described it at great length in several letters: "On the lovely isle of Hydra I actually saw Death. . . . I saw a skinless light, a naked brilliance and felt like I never felt before in my life. . . . death holds its warrant, a summoning to something wonderful and beautiful." For a long time Corso believed that the vision he had that morning was the very reason he had come to Greece in the first place. The following year he returned to Hydra and made a repeat visit to the exact spot where he'd had his vision. He reported the results to Ginsberg: "This time I went with no sorrow but with heavy breath. And excitement. The place is the only truly deserted enclosure of the whole island. And nothing happened." (At the time he made no notes except this: "What makes me see man as wonderful and victorious is in part my lack of seeing myself as so.")

2. Harold Norse. During his three years in Greece, Norse spent time living on "the enchanted islands" of Poros, Crete, Madouri, and Hydra. He indulged himself in boys, dancing, music, cannabis, and retsina before coming down with jaundice and hepatitis. On **Hydra** he befriended a then-unknown Canadian poet named Leonard Cohen, who would become famous as a singer-songwriter a few years later. Norse's cut-ups, such as "Sniffing Keyholes," inspired Cohen to become more innovative in his own prose, and his book *Beautiful Lovers* was the result.

Norse also spent a good deal of time on the island of **Madouri**, which was owned then by the Greek poet Nanos Valaoritis. Norse did nothing on Madouri but "sunbathe, wade in the blue-green water, and write poetry in the old mansion." Aristotle Onassis wanted to buy the island, but Valaoritis refused all his offers. At one point Onassis invited Norse to meet Greta Garbo on board his magnificent yacht, but Norse had made other commitments and never met the reclusive actress.

Harold Norse in Crete, 1964

Photo by Charles Henri Ford

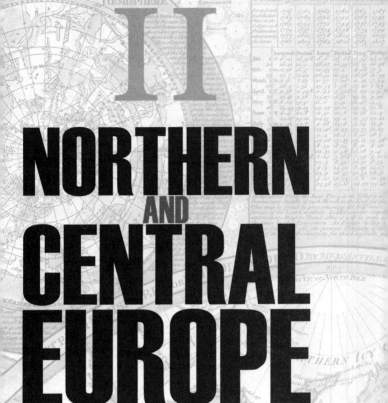

II

NORTHERN AND CENTRAL EUROPE

England

LONDON

1. Jack Kerouac. It was in September 1943, during World War II, that Jack Kerouac made his first trip to London. He was on shore leave from the Merchant Marines while his ship, the S.S. *George Weems*, was being unloaded in Liverpool. After attending a concert of Tchaikovsky's music at the Royal Albert Hall, Kerouac explored Piccadilly Circus, where he and his fellow crew members got drunk and found prostitutes. He was only in London for a day, but managed to see Lord Nelson's statue and visit Hyde Park between pints of warm ale. Back on board ship he finished reading John Galsworthy's *The Forsyte Saga*, a crucial inspiration for him to conceive of his own writing as a single epic story about his life and family.

Kerouac made a second trip to London in April 1957 after visiting Burroughs in Tangier to help assemble the manuscript for *Naked Lunch*. On this trip, Kerouac stayed with his friend Seymour Wyse at his apartment [**33 Kingsmill Terrace**]. Writing to Ginsberg, he recommended a cheap "cubicle" room at the Mapleton Hotel [now called the Thistle Hotel, **39 Coventry Street**] near Piccadilly Circus. While in England Kerouac made an outline for his next novel, *The Dharma Bums*. On Good Friday he sat in St. Paul's Cathedral and with tears streaming down his face he listened to the hauntingly beautiful music of Bach's *St. Matthew Passion* performed by the St. Paul's choir and orchestra. Later Kerouac stopped in at the British Museum library, where he looked up his family in *Rivista Araldica* and found proof that Lebris de Keroack had emigrated to Canada from Brittany. The family motto was given as "Aimer, Travailler et Souffrir," or "Love, Work, and Suffer," as he translated it in *Lonesome*

Traveler. He also admired the paintings by El Greco in the National Gallery and toured Dr. Samuel Johnson's house at **17 Gough Square**. He even squeezed in a performance of *Antony and Cleopatra* at the Old Vic theatre [**103 The Cut**] after collecting an advance for his next book from his publisher, André Deutsch.

2. William S. Burroughs. William Burroughs lived in England off and on for many years. His first visit to London came in 1933, when he and David Kammerer made their European tour during a summer vacation from college, but his first extended trips began in 1956. By that time, Burroughs had become addicted to heroin. He learned that a doctor in London, Dr. John Yerbury Dent [**24 Addison Road**], was offering a two-week apomorphine program guaranteed to help kick the habit. Burroughs found that apomorphine was the only thing that was truly effective for him, and he wrote many enthusiastic articles and letters endorsing Dr. Dent's methods. By 1958 Burroughs had picked up a habit again and returned to the good doctor for a cure once more. By that time Dr. Dent had offices at **2 Mansfield Street**.

In 1959, Burroughs moved to London permanently and rented rooms at the Empress Hotel [**25 Lillie Road**] until 1961. It is now the site of the Hotel Lily and the Lillie Langtree Pub, a place where Burroughs dined occasionally. During this period Burroughs met Michael Portman, a good-looking and very wealthy seventeen-year-old who was an admirer of Burroughs' work. They formed a relationship that lasted for several years. When Burroughs returned to London in February 1962 he stayed again at the Empress Hotel, but in early March he moved into a basement apartment of his own at **5 Lancaster Terrace**. The following year Lawrence Ferlinghetti visited him here and described the room: "I go to see William Burroughs underground. . . . Two floors down, in a subbasement with

William Burroughs

no windows but a French door leading nowhere but onto a concrete triangular area like an airshaft. He says it's convenient for his cat who craps there. In the little room there is only a couch, a small table, a portable typewriter, no books in sight." It was a productive visit, and together they planned the publication by City Lights of *The Yage Letters*.

Every year or two Burroughs would return to London for extended visits interrupted by trips to Tangier, Paris, and New York. In 1964 he ran into difficulties when the British government decided that they would only give him an entry visa for two weeks due to his suspected drug use. On that short trip he was scheduled to appear on a television program, so he stayed at the Devonshire Hotel [**7 Princes Square**]. He soon managed to resolve his visa problems and was allowed to go back to his regular pattern of staying for six months at a time. In 1967 he lived at the Hotel Rushmore [**11 Trebovir Road, Earl's Court**], where he wrote *The Wild Boys*. His next address was **8 Duke Street, St. James**, where he lived for four years. Here Ian Sommerville and Alan Watson stayed with him for long periods of time and he produced several books, including *The Last Words of Dutch Schultz* and *Exterminator*.

3. Gregory Corso. Gregory Corso, who preferred Paris and Rome, spent less time in England. Corso's first trip to London came in 1958 when he visited with Allen Ginsberg on a reading trip. While in town the poets met Dame Edith Sitwell for lunch at the Sesame Club [**49 Grosvenor Street**], where she lived. She ordered for them. "Some very odd food," Gregory said. "Shrimps caught in frozen butter. She is real soul. Likes our poetry – and when we offered to turn her on she gracefully declined saying 'I fear I have been denied the joy of drugs – I once had morphine and became ill.'" In London they were asked to give interviews on the B.B.C., and in their spare time they watched the swans on the Thames and visited William Blake's grave in Bunhill Fields [**38 City Road**]. Above all, Corso was impressed with the paintings by J.M.W. Turner that he found in the museums. In the summer of 1961, Gregory moved to London and stayed at **13 Tite Street** for a while. By the fall he had moved to an apartment at **76 Regents Park Road** near the London zoo, a locale that inspired his short poem "Direction Sign in London Zoo":

Gregory Corso reading at Albert Hall, London, 1965

Giant Panda
Lions
Humming Birds
Ladies

While at that same address he worked on poems for his next New Directions book. Although he planned to call the collection *Apples,* it was changed at the last minute to *Long Live Man.*

4. Allen Ginsberg. On Allen Ginsberg's first trip to London in 1958, he traveled with Gregory Corso from Paris and stayed for a few weeks, doing readings, giving interviews, and visiting all the museums and historical sites he could. He would return to the city dozens of times, most importantly in the spring of 1965. Ginsberg had just been expelled from both Prague and Cuba but found himself warmly welcomed in London. By coincidence Bob Dylan was in town giving concerts at the **Royal Albert Hall** on May 9 and 10, so he invited Allen to see the shows. D.A. Pennebaker decided to make a short film

Allen Ginsberg reading at Albert Hall, London, 1965

Allen Ginsberg visiting William Blake's cottage in Feltham, 1979

Photo © Allen Ginsberg LLC

clip of Dylan singing "Subterranean Homesick Blues" in the alley behind the Savoy Hotel [**The Strand**] just off Savoy Place, and they asked Allen to make a cameo appearance in the background of the movie, dressed as an old Jewish man. Seeing Dylan's sold-out concert gave Allen the impetus to try and do the same thing with poets, and the Albert Hall was rented for a mammoth reading on June 11. Corso, Ferlinghetti, Alex Trocchi, Charles Olson, and Barbara Guest all participated in the reading, and Andrei Voznesensky and Indira Gandhi were in the audience. The whole production was taped, and a film of the event called *Wholly Communion* was released later. It didn't quite sell the hall out like Dylan's concert, but 7,000 people did fill most of the auditorium. Ferlinghetti said that he saw "more jeans, longer hair, black turtlenecks than any reading in America." The epic event went on for four hours, until poets and audience alike were exhausted. During that same visit to London, Allen climbed to the top of the hill in **Primrose Hill Park** to enjoy the view. It inspired him to write his poem "Guru."

In July 1967, Ginsberg made a trip to read at the Queen Elizabeth Hall [**Southbank Centre, Belvedere Road**] with W.H. Auden, Charles Olson, Stephen Spender, and Giuseppe Ungaretti. But the real excitement of the trip came when Ginsberg was invited to watch Mick Jagger, Paul McCartney, and John Lennon record "Dandelion Fly Away." Allen, always star-struck, considered being present at that recording session one of the high points of his life. A few days later he took part in the Dialectics of Liberation Conference along with Stokely Carmichael, Paul Goodman, and Herbert Marcuse. Over the next thirty years, Allen made countless reading trips to London, always playing the role of tourist and visiting all the museums he could in whatever spare time he had. On his last appearance at the Royal Albert Hall in 1995 he appeared on stage with Anne Waldman, Tom Pickard, and Alice Notley, introducing the next generation of poets to the London audience. Paul McCartney, who was by then an old friend, also came on stage to perform "Ballad of the Skeletons" with Ginsberg.

5. Lawrence Ferlinghetti.

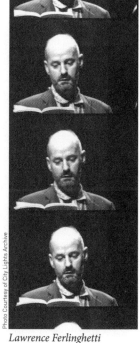

Photo Courtesy of City Lights Archive

Lawrence Ferlinghetti visited London many times for both business and pleasure. During World War II he spent a good deal of time here on leave from his naval assignments. Then in 1950 he stayed in London for a few days before leaving for America and his marriage to Kirby Selden. Images from his visits showed up in a poem in his first book, *Pictures of the Gone World*:

> London
> crossfigured
> creeping with trams
> and the artists on sundays
> in the summer
> all 'tracking Nature'
> in the suburbs

Lawrence Ferlinghetti reading at Albert Hall, London, 1965

Other poems, either written in London or based on London memories, would follow, including "London, Rainy Day," "The Situation in the West Followed by a Holy Proposal," and "A Giacometti Summer." In the sixties, he visited the **Tate Gallery** with Pablo Armando Fernández before going to see William Burroughs in his basement apartment on Lancaster Terrace to discuss publishing *The Yage Letters*. When he appeared at the famous **Royal Albert Hall** reading in 1965, Ferlinghetti was staying at a friend's apartment in King's Court North, **189 King's Road**.

6. Eric Mottram. Perhaps the most important academic supporter of alternative American literature in Europe was Eric Mottram (1924–1995). He was a professor of English and American Literature at King's College London [**Surrey Street**] from 1960 until his retirement in 1990. He is also the author of one of the best critical books on Burroughs' work, *The Algebra of Need*, and taught at many universities as a visiting professor, including several in the United States. Through his work he became friends with Ginsberg, Ferlinghetti, Burroughs, and many other Beat Generation writers.

Eric Mottram

Photo © Allen Ginsberg LLC

7. Others. Not surprisingly, nearly all the major Beat writers visited London at least once in their lives. Antony Balch, who worked with William Burroughs on several experimental films, including *Towers Open Fire* and *The Cut-Ups,* was born in London in 1937 and died here of stomach cancer in 1980. Neal Cassady's widow, Carolyn Cassady, moved to **5 Belsize Avenue** in London in the 1980s, remaining in England for the rest of her life. She summed up her move by saying that "London is the greatest city in the world for K.U.L.T.C.H.U.R. – of which California is devoid now."

Carolyn Cassady

EAST GRINSTEAD

1. William S. Burroughs. Throughout the sixties, William Burroughs took a very active interest in Scientology. At first he was convinced that the Scientologists had found a basic key to help unlock the secret of psychological and personality disorders, but eventually he came to believe that the founder of Scientology, L. Ron Hubbard, was more charlatan than saint. Between 1959 and 1966 the global headquarters for the Scientology movement was the 59-acre Saint Hill Manor [**Saint Hill Green**] in East Grinstead, about fifty miles from London. By mid-January 1968, when Burroughs took a two-month-long course at the center, Hubbard had moved his own headquarters elsewhere. Over the years Burroughs wrote several articles about the religious group, weighing the good and the bad. "The fact is," he wrote with great pragmatism, "that processing has uncovered a lot of extremely useable literary material and dreams now have a new dimension of clarity and narrative continuity. I have already made more than the money put out on stories and material directly attributable to processing. So might as well follow through and see what turns up."

TAPLOW

1. Brion Gysin. John Clifford, later known as Brion Gysin, was born in a Canadian military hospital in Taplow, near London, on January 19, 1916. His father, Leonard Samuel Gysin, was in the army during World War I and was killed at the bloody Battle of the Somme eight months after Brion's birth. Brion's mother, Stella Margaret Martin Gysin, returned to Edmonton, Canada, after this to raise her son. At the time of Brion's birth the military was using the Taplow House [**Berry Hill**], a beautiful Georgian manor, as its hospital. The site is now an elegant hotel.

GLASTONBURY

1. Janine Pommy Vega. Following a horrific automobile accident in 1982, writer Janine Pommy Vega went to Europe to restore her spirit as well as her health. Her book *Tracking The Serpent* describes the inner healing process she underwent as she explored prehistoric sites related to female deities, the earth goddesses of the past. At the top of her list was a visit to Glastonbury's famous **Tor**, and the ruin of **St. Michael's Church** on the summit, which she first glimpsed from the window of her bus. After checking

into a local bed-and-breakfast run by one Mrs. Kinsman, she climbed the Neolithic mound, awestruck by the "undulating pasture land, ending on three sides at a line of hills," she wrote. After visiting a number of similar locations in England, Ireland and France, as outlined in her book, she gradually recovered her health and her enthusiasm for life.

BATH

1. Brion Gysin. In September 1931, at the age of fifteen, Brion Gysin was sent to the Downside School [**Stratton-on-the-Fosse Radstock**]. It was known as the "Eton of Catholic public schools" and was run by the Benedictine monks of Downside Abbey. Gysin came to the school from his home in Edmonton, Canada, and he excelled in English literature, Chaucer and Shakespeare in particular. Here he edited the school magazine, *The Raven,* and was a member of the debating society. After he graduated in July 1934, Gysin didn't think about Downside very much, but his impressions of the religious brothers of the Abbey resurfaced in a 1947 short story he wrote about a monk who discovered an error in the calculation of time.

2. Ian Sommerville. On February 5, 1976, Ian Sommerville was killed in a car accident in Bath. He had just gotten his driver's license and was driving alone when he lost control of the car. Sommerville had been one of William Burroughs' closest friends and had helped Brion Gysin invent the Dreamachine. He also collaborated with Gysin and Burroughs on the book *Let the Mice In.* His death coincided with Burroughs' sixty-second birthday, and the shock of the accident threw Burroughs into a depression.

OXFORD

1. Allen Ginsberg and Gregory Corso. During the second week of May 1958, Allen Ginsberg and Gregory Corso came to Oxford to give a reading at New College [**Holywell Street**]. When Corso began to read his new poem, "Bomb," he was attacked by the students, some of whom jeered and threw shoes at him. They misunderstood the meaning of the poem and thought that Corso was promoting the use of the atomic bomb. In an era that feared nuclear annihilation, lines like, "You bomb | toy of universe Grandest of all snatched sky I cannot hate you," and "O Bomb I love you | I want to kiss your clank eat your boom," did not strike the listeners as ironic. On the same trip Corso and Ginsberg visited W.H. Auden, who gave them a tour of the town, pointing out all the places he remembered from his days as a young schoolboy. That afternoon when Gregory playfully asked him, "Are birds spies?" Auden replied, "No, I don't think so, who would they report to?" To which Allen said, "The trees."

CAMBRIDGE

1. Ian Sommerville and William S. Burroughs. In 1959, when Ian Sommerville met William Burroughs at the Mistral Bookshop in Paris, he was on summer holiday from his university studies at Cambridge. His specialty there was mathematics and electronics. When Brion Gysin asked him to help invent a machine to use in their experiments with the effects of flickering light on the brain, Sommerville came up with what they would later call the Dreamachine. He pinpointed the date of the invention as February 15, 1960. Burroughs visited his friend and sometime lover in Cambridge several times during his senior year, and in November 1960, Burroughs, Gysin and Sommerville put on a multimedia display combining painting, poetry and slide projections for the Heretics Club of Corpus Christi College in Cambridge. "I prefer Cambridge to London and find I can accomplish more here as regards work and contacts," Burroughs wrote. At the time he felt he had no prospect of an English sale of *Naked Lunch,* and was waiting for Grove to publish it in the U.S. While staying in Cambridge, Burroughs took "a palatial room overlooking the market for four £ per week with breakfast." His quarters were in St. Mary's Chambers on **St. Mary's Passage, just off Market Mill**. Although lodgings were cheap, meals were dreadful. He wrote to a friend, "The food in Cambridge is all time low in all my experience as traveler I turn sick with the thought of the meal that waits for me cold and soggy in all the restaurants."

NEWCASTLE UPON TYNE

1. Basil Bunting. A Northumbrian poet who had been a friend of Ezra Pound and Louis Zukofsky, Basil Bunting lived about twenty minutes from Newcastle at **Shadingfield, Wylam**. In May 1965 his admirer Allen Ginsberg visited him there, provided with an introduction by fellow poets Tom Pickard and Jonathan Williams, who also had the highest regard for Bunting. Bunting's long poem "Briggflatts" was to be published that year by the Fulcrum Press, and he and Ginsberg gave a reading together in Newcastle. In 1978, when Bunting was seventy-eight years old, Allen used his influence to raise money to help support the poverty-stricken elder poet. He is buried in the Quaker cemetery at Briggflatts, Cumbria.

Allen Ginsberg and Basil Bunting, Newcastle, 1965

2. Tom Pickard. In 1964, poet Tom Pickard and his wife, schoolteacher Connie Watson, founded a poetry center in the ancient Morden Tower, still located on **Back Stowell Street, West Walls**. They sponsored readings for Alexander Trocchi, Robert Creeley, Basil Bunting, Lawrence Ferlinghetti, Gregory Corso, and Tom Pickard himself. Allen Ginsberg read at Morden Hall on several occasions, calling it "celestially decorous, a medieval tur-

ret wherein youthful bards, in poetic tatterdemalion, or spiritual colored dress, with manly hair princely-long, wine cups or other alchemic potions at hand, their lasses sensitive tender and observant, in the center of Satanic-architectured city in Albion."

Tom Pickard

Scotland

EDINBURGH

1. William S. Burroughs. One of the first major literary events that William Burroughs participated in was a five-day Writers' Conference that took place in McEwan Hall on **Teviot Place** as part of the Edinburgh International Festival held in August 1962. The English publisher John Calder helped organize the event and invited Burroughs to take part; the roster also included American writers Mary McCarthy, Norman Mailer, and Henry Miller, as well as British writers Lawrence Durrell, Stephen Spender, and Alexander Trocchi. The conference was reported widely in the media and attracted crowds that filled the

2,300-seat auditorium to overflowing, especially for the final day's panel about censorship. At one point Burroughs' work was attacked by Spender and Hugh MacDiarmid. MacDiarmid blustered to the press that the literature of Burroughs and Trocchi was "all heroin and homosexuality. These people belong in jail, not on the lecture platform." Mailer and McCarthy rushed to Burroughs' defense, countering that books like *Naked Lunch* were the only interesting contemporary works worth reading.

GLASGOW

1. Helen Adam and Alexander Trocchi. Two writers associated with the Beat Generation were born in Glasgow. The first was Helen Adam, born here on December 2, 1909. As a young woman she moved to the United States in 1939, eventually winding up in San Francisco, where she became an active member of the San Francisco Renaissance. She practiced writing in ballad form and used performance techniques as part of her readings. In San Francisco she counted Robert Duncan, Jess, and Jack Spicer among her close friends and got along well with many of the Beat writers.

Alexander Trocchi was born in Glasgow on July 30, 1925, the son of a Scottish mother and an Italian father. After attending the University of Glasgow, he moved to Paris in the 1950s, where he edited a magazine called *Merlin,* which attracted the attention of the literary community. Many of Trocchi's novels were published by Maurice Girodias' Olympia Press under pseudonyms. He was friendly with many of the American Beat writers then living in Paris, and spent time at the Beat Hotel with William Burroughs and Brion Gysin. After becoming hooked on heroin, he wrote about drug addiction in his most famous novel, *Cain's Book.* Trocchi passed away in London in 1984.

Wales

CARDIFF

1. Lawrence Ferlinghetti. Ferlinghetti's poem "Spirit of the Crusades" was inspired by a trip to Cardiff:

> Stoney Wales
> with its slate-grey roofs
> in slate-grey Cardiff
> and its greystone houses on greystone terraces
> and its great high statue of
> "The Spirit of the Crusades" in the Wales National
> Museum . . .

He saw the statue in question in the National Museum of Cardiff [**Cathays Park**]. Sculpted by artist Alice Meredith Williams, it shows a mounted crusader from the Middle Ages incongruously surrounded by World War I era doughboys.

SWANSEA

1. Allen Ginsberg and Dylan Thomas. In 1995 Allen Ginsberg visited Wales for an appearance at the United Kingdom's Year of Literature and Writing Festival. It was held in the refurbished Swansea Guildhall, which that year had been turned into the Dylan Thomas Centre in honor of the famous Welsh poet. Thomas was born in Swansea in 1914, and few poets of the twentieth century were more influential than he. Ginsberg had met Dylan Thomas and heard him read in the 1950s, so Swansea was a point of interest for him. To a friend he wrote, "saw Dylan Thomas' boat house (big place) and tiny writing shack overlooking vast bay near Swansea at Laugharne."

BLACK MOUNTAINS

1. Allen Ginsberg. In July 1967, after appearing at the International Dialectics of Liberation Conference in London, Allen Ginsberg was invited by his British publisher, Tom Maschler, to stay at his home in the Black Mountains of Wales. While sitting on a hillside overlooking the dramatic Welsh countryside, Ginsberg took some LSD and composed a Wordsworthian landscape poem called "Wales Visitation." Allen considered it to be one of his best efforts. He wrote about the nature surrounding him, the lambs and cows and the fog drifting over the mountains. It begins:

> White fog lifting & falling on mountain-brow
> Trees moving in rivers of wind
> The clouds arise
> as on a wave, gigantic eddy lifting mist
> above teeming ferns exquisitely swayed
> along a green crag
> glimpsed thru mullioned glass in valley raine—

THE NETHERLANDS

AMSTERDAM

1. Gregory Corso and Simon Vinkenoog. The earliest Beat visitor to The Netherlands was Gregory Corso. While he was living in Paris in 1957, he passed some bad checks and then fled the city for fear that his creditors would catch up with him. He wound up hiding out in Amsterdam for about two months, staying at **Reijnier Vinckeleskade 80**, in a house that once stood across the street from the ca-

Steven Taylor, Allen Ginsberg, and Peter Orlovsky

nal. Allen Ginsberg and Peter Orlovsky arrived in Paris a few weeks later, expecting to find Corso there, and ended up having to track him down in Amsterdam. During their stay in Amsterdam they made friends with Simon Vinkenoog, a well-known Dutch poet and writer who would become their Dutch translator. Vinkenoog would work with the Beats until his death in 2009. In 2004 he was selected Poet Laureate of The Netherlands.

Many Beat writers stayed with Vinkenoog and his family in their home during their reading tours. Beginning in the late seventies, Ginsberg performed annually at De Kosmos nightclub in Amsterdam, and he always stayed with Simon. On the last major trip that Allen Ginsberg and Peter Orlovsky took together, a 1983 European tour with musician Steven Taylor, the trio met in Amsterdam to produce a recording. By that time, Orlovsky was in dire straits due to mental illness and drugs, and he created havoc wherever he went. He terrorized Vinkenoog's family, and this convinced Ginsberg that they could no longer travel together.

Dutch translator Simon Vinkenoog with two of his children and Allen Ginsberg

DENMARK

COPENHAGEN

1. William S. Burroughs. The first of William Burroughs' two visits to Copenhagen was in the late summer of 1957, when he spent about a month with his oldest friend, Kells Elvins, and Elvins' third wife, the Danish actress Mimi Heinrich. Burroughs stayed in a hotel in the city and visited Kells in his house in the smaller town of Mikkelborg. In Copenhagen Burroughs worked on the Freeland section of *Naked Lunch*, satirizing what he felt was the oppressive sterility of Scandinavian socialism. "I reach Freeland," he writes, "which is clean and dull my God." Later he wrote of Copenhagen, "If a citizen wanted anything from a load of bone meal to a sexual partner, some department was ready to offer effective aid." Additional material based on his impressions of Copenhagen found their way into two of his cut-up novels, *The Ticket That Exploded* and *Nova Express*.

In the sixties Burroughs contemplated moving to Copenhagen, but he did not return until October 1983, when he came back with his friend and companion James Grauerholz. On this trip he gave a series of performances and readings. He visited The Book Trader bookstore at **Skindergade 23** for an interview and gave a reading at the Saltlageret theater, which has since been torn down and replaced by the Tycho Brahe Planetarium [**Gl. Kongevej 10**]. That ageless performance was captured on film in *Words of Advice*.

GERMANY

BERLIN

1. Gregory Corso. In July of 1959 Gregory Corso took his first trip to Berlin. He had been invited to read at the Technische Universität Berlin [**Strasse des 17 Juni 135**] by his translator and collaborator Walter Höllerer. Corso loved Berlin at first, especially East Berlin, which he found "vast and desolate, yet somewhat gentle." Höllerer lived in a pleasant, quiet house at **Heerstrasse 99**.

In the fall of 1960, Corso returned to Berlin and stayed for several months. He got to know the city, both West and East, and gave another reading at the Technical University where Höllerer taught. "It was bombed and is augmented by new glass structure – old & new entwined – very odd to see," Gregory said, describing the area around the school. A giant statue of Joseph Stalin impressed him too, but it was "less graceful than the Hercules across from him on the gymnasium steps," he wrote. The zoo in West Berlin was open to East and West Berliners alike, and it inspired Gregory, who wrote:

East is East
West is West
Berlin has both
And both is best

The divided city inspired an idea that stuck with him for the rest of his life. "When faced with a choice," he frequently said, "choose both."

Corso and Höllerer got along well, and together they edited a large anthology of American poetry, which they called *Junge Amerikanische Lyrik* one of the first international publications to feature the Beat Generation writers as a group. It was published in 1961 by Carl Hanser in Munich and included one of the earliest audio recordings of Beat writers. Corso was very productive in Berlin, composing quite a lot of poetry, editing the German anthology, and writing many letters.

2. Lawrence Ferlinghetti. In February 1967, Lawrence Ferlinghetti flew to Berlin to read at the Berlin Literary Colloquium. Nearly 5,000 people attended the reading he gave with Russian poet Andrei Voznesensky. Contrary to Corso's feelings about East Berlin, Ferlinghetti found it to be a "joyless civilization," and he described the Berlin Wall as a "monster serpent running thru the city, like some kind of barbaric medievalism." Afterwards, images of Berlin crept into his poetry. "Two wrongs make a right in Berlin | Unter den Linden | by Brandenburg Gate" he wrote in a poem titled "Berlin." While in Germany

Lawrence Ferlinghetti at Berlin Festival, 2004

Photo Courtesy of City Lights Archive

Ferlinghetti began work on a sequel to his novel *Her*, tentatively titled *Berlin Blue Rider*, which never developed beyond several pages of notes.

Lawrence spent his time in West Berlin with friend and interpreter Heiner Bastian, who was translating his poetry for *Akzente* magazine. Among their escapades, Lawrence has claimed that one night at three a.m., the two of them switched all of the shoes that had been set outside the doors in the hotel corridor to be cleaned and shined. The results of this Great Shoe Exchange have been sadly lost to history, but Ferlinghetti speculated about performing a repeat operation on the other side of the Iron Curtain: "If we did it in the Hotel Metropol, Moscow, it would be a real test of Communism—the people waking in the morning must, if they are good Communists, put on whosoever's shoes they find in front of their door & walk off, happy & interchangeable. . . ."

3. ruth weiss. Poet ruth weiss (who eschewed the use of upper case letters in her name) was born in Berlin in 1928. Her father was a journalist and worked as the night editor for a Berlin-based news service, but lost his job due to the rise of German Nationalism. The family left to live in Vienna and then Holland, keeping one step ahead of the Nazis. They finally escaped in 1939, when ruth was just ten years old. Her family fled to the United States, settling first in New York before eventually winding up in San Francisco.

4. Others. In 1983, while teaching in Berlin at the Deutscher Akademischer Austrauschdienst [offices at **Markgrafenstrasse 37**] with writer in residence Ted Joans, Robert Creeley stayed in an apartment at **Storkwinkel 12** for several months. Joans was his neighbor here and they often took short trips together and visited the beach at Wannsee in the southwestern part of the city. Creeley often lamented the fact that he was entirely unable to learn German (or any other foreign language, for that matter). This hampered him quite a bit during his travels. He wrote about Berlin in his short "Letter from Berlin," which appears in his *Collected Essays*.

Allen Ginsberg visited Berlin on several occasions to give readings. Once in 1976 he spent a memorable afternoon having cocktails with Samuel Beckett.

ANDERNACH

1. Charles Bukowski. Although not a Beat writer by most definitions, Charles Bukowski is often grouped together with them. He was born in Andernach on August 16, 1920, and lived in nearby Pfaffendorf until he was three. Bukowski's father was a U.S. Army sergeant stationed in Andernach during World War I, who stayed on as a building contractor after his tour of duty, hoping to make a living on postwar German reconstruction projects. He married a German woman, Katharina Fett, and before long, Heinrich Karl Bukowski (later to be called Charles) was born. 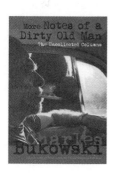 In April 1923, the family relocated to America, settling permanently in the Los Angeles area. Bukowski's writings are tremendously popular in Germany, just as Bob Kaufman's are popular in France. Bukowski, himself, could give no reason for this regional popularity.

FRANKFURT

1. Gregory Corso. Frankfurt was the scene of one of Gregory Corso's few attempts to hold down a regular job. In January 1958, in midwinter, Corso left Paris in order to sell Collier's encyclopedias to U.S. servicemen stationed in Frankfurt. He realized quickly that he was ill-suited for the job of taking advantage of people by selling them things they didn't need. He quit on his second day, after visiting the soldiers at the Gibbs Barracks, and within a few days went right back to Paris. "I was almost not a poet but a Collier's representative," he wrote to Ginsberg. One thing that he did enjoy during his brief stint in Frankfurt were the many night clubs where American rock 'n' roll was already popular.

HAMBURG

1. Allen Ginsberg. In June 1988, Robert Wilson, the American director and theatrical designer, produced a jazz opera in Hamburg based on the poetry of Allen Ginsberg. Composed by George Gruntz and conducted by Rolf Liebermann, it was called *Cosmopolitan Greetings*. Allen was on hand for the premiere at the Hamburg State Opera [**Grosse Theaterstrasse 25**]. In 1990, Wilson returned to Hamburg with his production of William S. Burroughs' *The Black Rider: The Casting of the Magic Bullets*. This time the music was composed by Tom Waits and the opera was performed in Hamburg's Thalia Theater [**Alstertor 1**].

HEIDELBERG

1. William S. Burroughs and Carl Weissner. On June 5, 1966, William Burroughs arrived in Heidelberg to visit Carl Weissner, who lived at **1-3 A Muhltastrasse**. Weissner had translated and edited several of Burroughs' works and shared his interest not only in the cut-up method but also in tape-recorded cut-ups, apomorphine, and Scientology. Along with Burroughs and the French poet/translator Claude Pélieu, Weissner collaborated on the pamphlet *So Who Owns Death TV?* which was published in 1967 by Pélieu's publishing company, Beach Books Texts and Documents. Weissner also published several of the Beat writers during the mid-sixties in his own periodical, *Klactoveedsedsteen*. In addition to championing the Beats, Weissner was a key figure in the translation of Charles Bukowski's works into German. Weissner passed away at his home on January 24, 2012.

MUNICH

1. Allen Ginsberg. In September 1957 Allen Ginsberg and Peter Orlovsky made their first visit to Munich, exploring the Dachau concentration camp a few miles northwest of the city. In his letters Allen noted that the area around the furnaces still showed traces of black ash, the only remains of thousands of unidentified victims; he was overwhelmed by the solitude of the camp. While in Munich Allen and Peter stayed with a friend who drove them around the city and took them to a giant beer garden and a jazz spot known as The Owl. Ginsberg returned many times over the next forty years, most notably in

Allen Ginsberg at the Lowenbrau Beer Hall, Munich

December 1979, when he performed at the Loft nightclub. The recording of the reading he gave here was turned into a successful record called *Gaté*. His German publisher Hanser Verlag had offices at **Kolbergerstrasse 22**, and Allen dropped in on each trip to Munich. In 1993 he visited for a week but ended up sick with bronchitis and stayed in his room at the Hotel an der Oper [**Falkenturmstrasse 10**] most of the time. Though unwell, he still managed to visit the Alte Pinakothek art museum [**Barer Strasse 27**] to see the old masters he loved so much.

2. Gregory Corso. In the summer of 1959 Gregory Corso gave a reading at the university in Munich, but the 100 marks he was paid didn't last him long, and soon enough he was writing desperate letters to his friends asking for money. He reported that he was sleeping outdoors in an English garden amid the rabbits and had nothing to eat for days at a time. Poet and millionaire James Merrill was in town, and Gregory managed to cadge a few dollars from him. He had a long discussion with the German translator of Pound and cummings, Eva Hesse, who lived at **Franz-Josef Strasse 7**. Finally, after a month of meager living, he scraped together enough money for a ticket to Venice, where he knew that he could count on Alan Ansen for free lodgings.

SWITZERLAND

LAUSANNE

1. Timothy Leary. Allen Ginsberg first met Timothy Leary in 1960 when Leary was still a relatively conservative psychology professor at Harvard. Leary had invited Allen to participate in some experiments he was con-

Timothy Leary and Neal Cassady, 1964

ducting with psilocybin in hopes that it could be used to treat mentally ill patients. Within a few years, Leary and Ginsberg had moved on to champion the general use of psychedelics, and jumpstarted a movement that was to sweep the country. Eventually Leary wound up in prison for the possession of illegal drugs. In 1970, he made a dramatic escape from a California jail and, with the help of a radical group called The Weathermen, he and his wife Rosemary fled to Algeria and from there to Switzerland. The Learys stayed with (perhaps a euphemism for "were held hostage by") wealthy arms dealer Michel Hauchard in his luxurious home in **Ouchy**, a lakeside resort town near Lausanne. Hauchard helped them rent their own villa in **Villars-sur-Ollon** and later a chalet in **Immensee** on Lake Zug. This life of luxury (and limited liberty) on the lam was not to last forever. United States Attorney General John Mitchell persuaded Switzerland to put Leary in Lausanne's Prison du Bois-Mermet [**Escaliers du Marché 4**], where he stayed for several weeks. During this period, Allen Ginsberg organized an appeal to have Leary released, issuing a petition titled *Declaration of*

Independence for Dr. Timothy Leary. Eventually the Swiss government decided not to extradite Leary, but by then he had soured on Switzerland as a refuge.

After his release, Leary traveled through Austria and Lebanon, finding himself dubbed "the most dangerous man in America" by President Richard Nixon. He ended up in Afghanistan, where he was finally captured and brought back to the United States in 1973.

HAUTE-NENDAZ

1. William S. Burroughs. In the fall of 1971, William S. Burroughs was invited to teach at the University of the New World, an alternative school situated in the mountains above Lake Geneva. The school put Burroughs up at the Résidence Monte-Calme [**Rte de la Télécabine, 3**], but he soon realized that the university was going broke and he would not be paid for teaching. Fearing that he would even be stuck footing his own hotel bill, he debated returning to England. "None the less very glad I came to see some sun and sky for a change and can't understand how I have stood London all this time. And the students are a gas," he wrote. Burroughs liked life in Switzerland, partly for predictable reasons: "Civilized country thank God codethyline in the drug stores name here is Neo-Codion. Same formula as the French product in fact this comes from France. I couldn't have got myself out of bed without it." Timothy Leary lived nearby and Burroughs went to visit him occasionally. He spent vast amounts of time reading science fiction, discovering a great passion for Frank Herbert's book *Dune*, which he recommended to all his students. In November the school did go out of business and Burroughs returned to London. Later he considered moving to Switzerland permanently. "Switzerland is cool enough with all those snow capped mountains and a citizen army where every man has a machine gun in his house and no causalities. But they are making it more and more difficult for outsiders to settle. They want to <u>keep</u> it cool," he complained.

ZURICH

1. Robert Frank. One of the twentieth century's greatest photographers, Robert Frank, was born in Zurich on November 9, 1924. As a young man in 1947 he emigrated to the United States, and by the mid-fifties he had become friends with many of the Beat writers. In 1959 he filmed *Pull My Daisy,* a black-and-white movie documenting a day in the life of the Beat Generation. The story was based on Jack Kerouac's play *Beat Generation,* and the film featured Allen Ginsberg, Peter Orlovsky, Gregory Corso, David Amram, Larry Rivers, and others, with narration by Kerouac. Ten years later Frank made another film called *Me and My Brother,* which tracked Peter Orlovsky's mentally ill brother Julius as he traveled around with Ginsberg and Orlovsky. Frank's seminal work *The Americans* had its American edition published in 1959 with an introduction by Jack Kerouac. When Allen Ginsberg renewed his own interest in photography during the 1980s, he sought Robert Frank's advice, and Robert was the last friend to visit Allen the day before his death in 1997.

Robert Frank

121

LIECHTENSTEIN

VADUZ

1. William S. Burroughs. In 1973 William Burroughs sold his entire archive to the financier Roberto Altman in Vaduz, Liechtenstein. He estimated that it took up thirty-five square feet and weighed 500 pounds. At the time of the sale Burroughs was considering moving either to Liechtenstein or to Scotland, but he said that the buyer didn't want him in their tiny country. In a letter Burroughs wrote a short routine about it: "My plans are confused as the earth shrinks in a heaving sea of air hammers. I had intended to establish myself in Lichtenstein but the billionaires are packed in shoulder to shoulder and cried out with one voice: 'You Can't Come In Here There Simply Isn't Room.' Question: Room for one more inside sir? Answer: NO!" The unfortunate part of the sale was that Burroughs didn't have free access to the archive and couldn't get at material he needed for future work, so he was relieved when the papers were later sold to an American collector. The archive eventually wound up in the Berg Collection at the New York Public Library, where it is available to all researchers.

AUSTRIA

VIENNA

1. William S. Burroughs. After William Burroughs graduated from Harvard in June 1936, he began receiving a monthly allowance of $200 from his wealthy parents to spend as he saw fit, and he decided to take a tour of Europe. There he found his way to Vienna, which he made his base of operations for a while. His biographer, Ted Morgan, writes, "[Burroughs was] captivated by the splendors of that great baroque city—the cathedral, the opera, the beaches on the Danube, the famous bath called the Romanische Baden, which was swarming with beautiful young boys." William decided to stay in Vienna at the Dianabad Hotel (torn down in 1967) and enroll in medical school at the University of Vienna [**Ringstrasse**] beginning that fall. He spent the next six months attending classes, visiting the Prater amusement park in the **Leopoldstadt** district (whose giant Ferris wheel was made famous by Orson Welles in his 1949 film *The Third Man*), and battling syphilis. As a homosexual he feared a Nazi takeover of Austria, and after undergoing an emergency operation for appendicitis at the Sanatorium Hera, he finally decided the time was ripe to leave.

CROATIA

DUBROVNIK

1. William S. Burroughs. In the summer of 1936, during his post-college tour of Europe, William S. Burroughs arrived in Dubrovnik with a letter of introduction to Ilse Klapper (1900–1982), a woman who had fled Germany in 1934 as the Nazis were coming to power. William liked her, and she showed him the best beaches and Gypsy cafés in town. The following year, after William dropped out of medical school in Vienna, he returned to Dubrovnik to recuperate from surgery and saw Klapper again. Her Yugoslavian visa was running out, and as a Jew in Europe her life was in danger. She persuaded Burroughs to marry her so that she could escape to America. They went to Athens in July 1937, where the ceremony took place at the U.S. Consulate, much to the disappointment of Burroughs' parents. This allowed Ilse to emigrate to New York City in 1939, where she worked as a secretary to the dramatist Ernst Toller. Although Burroughs never lived with her, they remained friends and saw each other whenever William was in New York. They divorced after the war in 1946.

2. Others. Over the years many other poets and writers who visited Dubrovnik were escorted by the translator

Vojo Šindolić, who calls the city his home. Allen Ginsberg and Peter Orlovsky stayed for a week inside the old walled city at the Hotel Dubravka [**Gundulić Square**]. In 1984, Michael McClure spent a few days with Šindolić at Vojo's parents' home. Here McClure wrote:

Michael McClure

Photo by Larry Keenan

THE OCEAN SCHURRS AND SLUSHES
and slurs like Jack said
and I hear it
here in the city of Dubrovnik
meaning
"little
grove" . . .

MACEDONIA

STRUGA

1. Allen Ginsberg. In August 1986, Allen Ginsberg was awarded the golden wreath at the Struga Festival.

He was honored by the prize, but didn't know exactly what to do with the solid gold laurel wreath housed in a special presentation box. He was much happier with the beautiful bilingual (Macedonian/English) edition of his poetry, published for the occasion. Ginsberg's poem "Cosmopolitan Greetings" was written especially to read at the award ceremonies. It begins with a poet's call to arms:

> Stand up against governments, against God.
> Stay irresponsible.
> Say only what we know & imagine.
> Absolutes are coercion.
> Change is absolute.
> Ordinary mind includes eternal perceptions.
> Observe what's vivid.
> Notice what you notice.
> Catch yourself thinking . . .

III
EASTERN EUROPE

CZECH REPUBLIC

PRAGUE

1. Allen Ginsberg. One of the major events in the life of Allen Ginsberg came on May Day 1965, when he was elected the King of May (Kral Majales) in Prague. Ginsberg had arrived in Czechoslovakia that February, fresh from his expulsion from Cuba, where his comments about politics and homosexuality had been deemed too controversial for Castro's government. Allen was determined to keep a low profile in the then-Communist city of Prague. He stayed here quietly for several weeks before traveling to Russia and Poland, and then arrived back in Prague at the end of April, planning to stay for a few more weeks before returning home. But Ginsberg was not a man destined to remain innocuous and invisible. While watching the local university students celebrate May Day, Ginsberg was surprised to be spontaneously elected May King and paraded through the city streets seated on a float with a crown on his head. Before the day was over, 10,000 people had joined in to cheer his coronation as ruler of the bacchanal. Despite the fact that he'd gotten embroiled unintentionally, it so upset the Czech government that they had him expelled. The secret police came to his hotel and es-

Allen Ginsberg as the King of May, Prague, 1965

Allen Ginsberg, Václav Havel, and Nanao Sakaki in Prague, 1990

corted him to the airport. That day, as he flew to London, he penned one of his best poems, "Kral Majales," which begins with the lines:

> And the Communists have nothing to offer but fat
>   cheeks and eyeglasses and lying policemen
> and the Capitalists proffer Napalm and money in
>   green suitcases to the Naked,
> and the Communists create heavy industry but the
>   heart is also heavy
> and the beautiful engineers are all dead, the secret
>   technicians conspire for their own glamour
> in the Future, in the Future, but now drink vodka
>   and lament the Security Forces,
> and the Capitalists drink gin and whiskey on air-
>   planes but let Indian brown millions starve

Twenty-five years later, after the fall of Communism, Allen flew back to Prague accompanied by fellow poets

Anne Waldman, Nanao Sakaki, and Andy Clausen. By then, Václav Havel, a Czech poet and playwright, had been elected president of Czechoslovakia, and he and Ginsberg became friends, often sharing coffee at the Cafe Viola [**Nové Město, Hybernská 24**]. On May 1, 1990, the city fathers restored Allen's crown as the King of May, and he read his latest poem, "Return Of Kral Majales," to an enthusiastic Czech crowd.

POLAND

KRAKÓW

1. Allen Ginsberg. While Allen Ginsberg was behind the Iron Curtain in 1965, he visited Poland and spent a week in Kraków, "which hath a beauteous Cathedral with giant polychrome altarpiece by medieval woodcarver genius Veit Stoss," he wrote. That masterpiece is on the high altar of Bazylika Mariacka (St. Mary's Basilica) [**Plac Mariacki 5**] in Kraków. While in Kraków he hitched a ride to the concentration camp at Auschwitz with some scout leaders. While Allen visited the site of the atrocities and had his picture taken under the "Arbeit Macht Frei" sign, he reported that the men he had come with tried to pick up schoolboys who were hanging around the barbed wire gazing at the tourists.

Ginsberg at Auschwitz Concentration Camp, 1965

WARSAW

1. Allen Ginsberg. On his trip to Poland in 1965, Allen Ginsberg stayed in Warsaw for three weeks at the Europejski Hotel [**Krakowskie Przedmiescie 13**]. Allen was a guest of the Ministry of Culture during the first week, and he paid for the next two weeks' lodging with his Polish translation royalties. "I stayed alone mostly or drank with a young Rimbaud-ish Marlon Brando writer at Writer's Union and long afternoons with editor of *Jazz* magazine who'd printed my poems, a Jewish good man who'd been in Warsaw Ghetto, escaped, and covered rest of war as journalist with Russian army and stood across river from Warsaw at end and saw the city destroyed by Germans and nationalist underground killed off," Ginsberg wrote in a letter. The former Jewish Ghetto was now a vast green space surrounded by new government housing projects with only a memorial to remind people of the extermination that had taken place here. The sadness of the monument, which shows the Jews facing the invisible legions of annihilation, brought Allen to tears. One night he met with the Russian poet Andrei Voznesensky, who was in town, and they were able to discuss literature and politics more freely than they could have in Moscow. Allen wrote several poems on this trip, including "Café in Warsaw" and "The Moments Return," which begins:

> a thousand sunsets behind tramcar wires in open
> skies of Warsaw
> Palace of Culture chinese peaks blacken against the
> orange-clouded horizon —
> an iron trolley rolling insect antennae sparks blue
> overhead, hat man limping past rusty apart-
> ment walls —

Christ under white satin gleam in chapels — trembling fingers on the long rosary — awaiting resurrection

BELARUS

MINSK

1. Allen Ginsberg. In November 1985, Allen Ginsberg went to Russia as a member of a literary delegation that included Arthur Miller, Susan Sontag, Harrison Salisbury, William Gaddis, Louis Auchincloss, and Norman Cousins. Their overprotective Soviet chaperones closely guided them through the cities of Minsk, Moscow, St. Petersburg, and Vilnius without allowing them the freedom to explore on their own. Still, they did manage to come in contact with many Soviet writers and, of course, bureaucrats. In Minsk the writers went en masse to the circus and saw various acrobats—"lions and dogs on ponies," Allen said. They were also taken to visit all the obligatory monuments and memorials to World War II soldiers, including The Great Patriotic War Museum [**Nezavisimosti pr. 25a**]

RUSSIA

MOSCOW

1. Allen Ginsberg. On his Eastern European tour in March 1965, Allen Ginsberg stopped in Moscow for two weeks as a guest of the Writers Union and met two Russian poets who would become lasting friends, Yevgeny

Allen Ginsberg and Andrei Voznesensky in photo booth

Yevtushenko and Andrei Voznesensky. Allen sat around **Red Square** talking to the writers, hearing "old gossip about Death," as he said. He kept busy by attending the ballet, the symphony, and several plays, and visiting many, many museums. His hotel was centrally located and he "passed thru Red Square every morning and evening and wrote poems in snow by the wall and stood there at midnight watching the guards yelling at Slavic lovers in GUM doorway [department store facing Red Square]." One day while he was here, Red Square became the scene of a gigantic parade for the Russian cosmonauts who had recently returned from outer space. For the last week of his stay, the Writer's Union upgraded his hotel room so that he looked out across the river at the Kremlin clock tower and the onion domes of St. Basil's Cathedral.

Late in 1985 Ginsberg returned to Moscow with a delegation of writers and read at Lomonosov University, part of the giant Moscow State University system. Yevtushenko and Andrei Sergeev acted as interpreters. Allen spent a good deal of time on the trip talking and sightseeing with Arthur Miller and his wife, photographer Inge Morath. The two writers shared similar political views and stirred up controversy by questioning the Russian government's imprisonment of several distinguished writer/activists.

Yevgeny Yevtushenko and Allen Ginsberg

Allen brought up the forbidden topic of gay liberation at one of the conference meetings, but no serious problems arose because of it. With Yevtushenko's help, Ginsberg was able to extend his visa by two weeks so that he could spend more time on his own in Russia as a tourist.

2. Lawrence Ferlinghetti. On February 9, 1967, Lawrence Ferlinghetti flew into Moscow from Berlin with the German translator Heiner Bastian, to spend a day before boarding the Trans-Siberian railroad. (Poet Andrei Voznesensky had pulled some strings with the Russian authorities to allow Ferlinghetti to move about the country more freely than the average tourist.) Ferlinghetti rode through the "great snow world and white birches in the gloaming" to the Hotel Metropol [**1/4 Teatralny Proyezd**]. Ginsberg had given him some addresses of people to look up, and in his brief time here he went to the Writers' Union at **52 Vorovsky** to meet Andrei Sergeev, who had translated the poetry of some of the Beat writers. Ferlinghetti noted that the portrait of Boris Pasternak was notably missing from their authors' gallery. In the evening he attended a theatrical adaptation of John Reed's *Ten*

Andrei Voznesensky and Lawrence Ferlinghetti, 1967

Days That Shook the World, staged at the Drama Theatre on **Taganka Square**. Most impressive was **Red Square**, where he wandered past the statue of poet Vladimir Mayakovsky. After his 9000-kilometer train ride (and various Siberian travails), Lawrence flew back to Moscow. From the airport into the city, under the influence of classical guitar music being piped into the bus, he penned one of his most beautiful poems, "Moscow in the Wilderness, Segovia in the Snow."

NEVEL

1. Naomi Ginsberg. Allen Ginsberg's mother, Naomi Livergant, was born in 1896 in Nevel, a small shtetl north of Vitebsk, near the current border with Belarus, in the center of the Pale of Russia. Like many Jewish families in the early twentieth century, the Livergants emigrated to New York's Lower East Side. When Allen visited Russia in 1965, he looked up one of his mother's relatives, Joe Levy, whose branch of the family had survived all the pogroms and wars and currently lived in Moscow. His cousin Joe was the first to tell Allen about his mother's dramatic life as a small girl in Nevel. In 1904, when Naomi was eight years old, Russia went to war with Japan and her father was drafted. Naomi's mother was in delicate health and unable to care for their four children by herself, and in order to survive, the family had to move into a cousin's small two-room cabin in Vitebsk, where assorted relatives helped take care of the children while Naomi's father Memele bribed his way onto a ship bound for America. A year later he had saved enough money to send for his family, and it was then that Allen's mother emigrated to New York City.

KHABAROVSK

1. Lawrence Ferlinghetti. Lawrence Ferlinghetti had dreamed of having some sort of an adventure in Russia. And so when in the early months of 1967, in the dead of winter, the opportunity presented itself to ride the Trans-Siberian railroad from one end of the vast country to the other, he jumped at it.

He went with the German poet and translator Heiner Bastian, repeating a trip that the French poet Blaise Cendrars had taken in the early years of the twentieth century. Staring out the window from the hermetically sealed sauna of the overheated train, he wrote in his journal, "The great Siberian Plain. It's like the sea – too huge

MOSCOW IN THE
WILDERNESS,
SEGOVIA IN THE
SNOW

by Lawrence Ferlinghetti

to write about – nothing but birch trees like the froth on endless white groundswells – sometimes thin lines of black forest on the horizon, forlorn towns, rail junctions, with switchmen standing outside of sentry houses . . . I had the strong feeling that I was going to freeze to death in the Mongolian Mountains." The far eastern town of Khabarovsk was the site of a daylong layover near the end of the voyage. Here Ferlinghetti stopped in a café and wrote the memorable short poem, "Recipe for Happiness in Khabarovsk or Anyplace":

> One grand boulevard with trees
> with one grand café in sun
> with strong black coffee in very small cups
> One not necessarily very beautiful
> man or woman who loves you
> One fine day.

NAKHODKA

1. Lawrence Ferlinghetti. At Nakhodka, the eastern terminus of the Trans-Siberian railroad, Ferlinghetti's Trans-Siberian adventures turned into misadventures. Here he planned to board a ship to Japan to visit Gary Snyder and then catch a plane back to San Francisco, but he was abruptly denied passage and booted off the ship for not having a proper Japanese visa. To add one woe on top of another, he fell ill with a serious fever and ended up hospitalized. Here in Nakhodka Ferlinghetti spent about a week in "Siberian exile," alone and sick, unable to proceed to Japan. Ultimately he was forced to fly all the way back to Moscow to catch a plane home. During his spell in limbo, Ferlinghetti wrote descriptions of this "forlorn port near Vladivostok" in his journal. Some highlights of the "miserable, brave new town of Nakhodka" included the bare hospital room, the propagandistic newspaper articles, and most of all the hotel dining room where he ate: "A long, narrow, ballroom-type scene, graced by a five-piece Western-type 'orchestra.' The musicians are all very serious in public, though they look like they might be 'cats' if allowed to escape for a few years. . . ."

IV
AFRICA

Tangier

The Moroccan city of Tangier, sometimes spelled as Tanger or Tangiers, was an exotic, mysterious place for most of the members of the Beat Generation. During the mid-twentieth century it had a reputation for an "anything goes" atmosphere that prompted many expatriates to settle here. Sitting at the western entrance to the Strait of Gibraltar, with Spain usually visible across the water, Tangier has been a crossroads for many cultures throughout its history. From the 1920s to the 1960s it was considered to have international status, divided into sections by foreign colonial powers. It attracted not just writers, but also spies, businessmen, entertainers, and diplomats. Drugs and young male prostitutes were readily available, which made it attractive to people like William Burroughs, Allen Ginsberg, Harold Norse, and Alan Ansen. The author Paul Bowles had settled in Tangier years before the Beats arrived, and he acted as something of a *paterfamilias* to the growing population of younger writers.

1. William S. Burroughs. Tangier is probably the city most associated with William Burroughs. An entire book could easily be written about the many years he spent in this ancient Moroccan port. When Burroughs fled Mexico City following the death of his wife, no other place in the world seemed to offer him as much as Tangier—drugs, boys, balmy climate, and of course a chance to keep clear of the Mexican prison system. He arrived at the beginning of January 1954 and had soon settled into the quiet, inexpensive, and uneventful life that he had been searching for. His initial reaction to the town was negative, and he thought that everyone was "shoving their noses into his business," but he soon mellowed. Shortly after

Paul Bowles, Gregory Corso, William Burroughs in Tangier, 1961

his arrival he discovered a cheap hotel called the Villa Muniria [**1 Calle Magallanes**], where he and many of his Beat friends would live off and on in the coming years. Burroughs stayed in other places as well during his time in Tangier, such as a room on **Place Amrah**, just below the kasbah, where he lived in 1956. It was at Villa Muniria that Burroughs began working on the prose routines that he called his *Word Hoard*, many of which would be collected in his most famous book, *Naked Lunch*.

During his first year in Tangier he met both Paul Bowles and Brion Gysin, two men who would become important friends over the next decade. It wasn't long before he also met a young boy named Kiki, who was living at **1 Calle de los Arcos**, a little alleyway behind the Socco Chico in the medina. For a few years the two were inseparable partners. The **Socco Chico** was to become the primary hangout for Burroughs and his friends, and they became everyday fixtures at the cafés on the small square.

While living in Tangier, Burroughs went through

several rounds of drug addiction and cures. In 1955 he went to the **Benchimol Hospital** to undergo one cure for his heroin addiction, with poor results, and the same year he tried an unsuccessful two-week sleep cure under the auspices of a certain Dr. Aptel, who was practicing in Tangier. (It wasn't until his discovery in 1956 of Dr. Dent's apomorphine cure in London that anything seemed to be effective.)

Photo © Allen Ginsberg LLC

William Burroughs

In the spring and summer of 1957, Burroughs became the magnet that attracted his other Beat friends to Tangier. They rendezvoused at the Villa Muniria to help him assemble the manuscript of *Naked Lunch,* which at that time was little more than a mass of typed sheets of paper randomly strewn about his room. Jack Kerouac was the first of the steady stream of guests to arrive, but he was followed by Allen Ginsberg, Peter Orlovsky, Alan Ansen, and others. They all lived in one room or another at the Muniria while they worked on the manuscript.

In 1961, his friends met again in Tangier. By this time Burroughs was involved with two younger boys, Ian Sommerville and Michael Portman, who really didn't fit in with most of his older friends. Burroughs had also become deeply involved with his recent cut-up experiments, working not only with words but photographs and audio tapes as well. His young new friends shared this interest, and he found little time for another reunion.

Hotel El Muniria, Tangier

Later in the fifties and sixties, while Burroughs was living in Paris and London, he would return each year to Tangier for months at a time, renting either an apartment or a house. In 1963–64 he had a house on the Marshan at **4 Calle Larache**, where he was bothered continually by his neighbors. They didn't object to Burroughs nearly as much as they hated his house-guests, Sommerville, Portman, and Gysin. They even attempted to put a curse on his house, something that Gysin at least firmly believed in. When Burroughs earned enough money to move to another location, he was glad to leave Calle Larache and his spell-casting neighbors behind.

2. Paul Bowles and Jane Bowles. Paul and Jane Bowles moved to Tangier in 1948 and remained here for the rest of their lives, enjoying a wide variety of addresses. As husband and wife, they lived rather separate lives and each had their own apartment. At one point Paul rented apartment 20 on the fourth floor of the **Immeuble Itesa** across from the American Consulate. Jane maintained apartment 15 on the floor immediately beneath Paul. However, it was their custom to eat together, and Jane would signal Paul when it was time for meals by tapping on her ceiling with a broomstick.

Brion Gysin became a close friend, and in the early 1950s Paul would often walk over to Brion's house in the casbah in the afternoons. They would either have tea here or go out to the Normandie cafe and sit and talk. One day while Bowles was living at the Hotel Massilia

[**11, Rue Targha**], recuperating from paratyphoid, William Burroughs came to meet him. "His manner was subdued to the point of making his presence in the room seem tentative," Bowles remembered. Bowles was in fact the connection who first introduced Burroughs to Brion Gysin.

Paul Bowles in Tangier, 1993

He was uneasy, however, about the influx of "beatniks" into Tangier. Paul was a very private person and felt that they would attract unwanted attention with some of their high-profile shenanigans. In May 1957, when he met Allen Ginsberg for the first time in Tangier, Allen didn't make a good impression. Ginsberg put his foot in his mouth when talking with Jane, who had just suffered a stroke. "Jane never forgave him for describing the effects of William Carlos Williams' stroke, and then suggesting that she learn Braille," Paul wrote.

In 1999 Paul died in the Italian Hospital in Tangier. (Jane had already passed away in a hospital in Spain in 1973.) The American Legation Museum [**8, rue d'Amérique**] in the old medina has an interesting display of materials related to the life of Paul Bowles, including his luggage decorated with an array of transit tags.

3. Brion Gysin. It was Paul Bowles who first suggested that Brion Gysin visit Tangier, because he knew that Brion would like the "strange and exotic" nature of

Brion Gysin

Photo Courtesy of City Lights Archive

Moroccan life. Invited for the summer, he eventually stayed for the better part of twenty-three years. In 1954, Gysin and Mohamed Hamri opened a restaurant called the 1001 Nights in **Dar Menebhi Palace** on the Marshan. It became "the" restaurant of choice for tourists and expatriates, with something to please everyone, from the local cuisine to the young dancing boys who performed nightly. The restaurant was a success in every way except financially: it went bankrupt in January 1958. William Burroughs ate here a couple of times, but he didn't know Gysin very well in those years. Later, in Paris, Gysin and Burroughs became the closest of friends, but during the early years in Tangier they rarely spoke.

In 1969 a friend of Gysin's, John Hopkins, took him for a ride on his motorcycle and they had an accident. Brion's foot was injured, and he had a toe amputated in the **Hospital Español**, where Bowles visited him.

4. Jack Kerouac. In February 1957, Jack Kerouac left New York for Tangier on an inexpensive Yugoslav freighter, the S.S. *Slovenija*. When he arrived, he rented a balcony apartment at the Villa Muniria for $20 a month. It had a beautiful view of the harbor and was several floors above Burroughs' garden apartment. It proved to be convenient for the work they were doing together. In *Desolation Angels* Kerouac wrote, "Immediately Bill Burroughs took me to the Casbah where the veiled women pass. He lives on a hill overlooking the bay where even now I can see the S.S. *Slovenija* docked. We smoke marijuana right in

Jack Kerouac on the beach in Tangier, 1957

the cafes, in public, it's legal – a strange wild Arab town – old as Time." Jack was a fast typist (as his own marathon bouts had proved), so he set to work putting Burroughs' manuscript of *Naked Lunch* into some semblance of order. Since Burroughs was reclusive, Jack spent a good deal of his time alone drinking cheap bottles of Cinzano and Malaga wine, taking walks in the evening through the oldest parts of the city. His most memorable experience was a hike he took to a Berber village in the mountains behind the city. "Grass-and-stick huts on slopes, sheep, cattle, fierce looking herdsmen with dark faces and turbans and bare knees, and beautiful Berber women with enormous packs on their backs toiling up the grade," he wrote in a letter to his agent, Sterling Lord. One of the peasants gave him a machete with a gold-braided handle. In *Lonesome Traveler* Kerouac writes about eating at Dutch Tony's bar, which was another popular spot frequented by writers.

By April 5, Kerouac was homesick and ready to move on. Ginsberg and Orlovsky had arrived by then, and had pitched in to help with the manuscript. So Jack sailed to

William Burroughs and Peter Orlovsky in Tangier, 1957

Allen Ginsberg and Peter Orlovsky in the mountains of Morocco, 1957

Marseilles to explore Europe on his own, and left the others to finish the work.

5. Allen Ginsberg and Peter Orlovsky. When Ginsberg first arrived in Tangier at the end of March 1957, he and Orlovsky lived in a small room in the Villa Muniria until Kerouac left on April 5, at which point they moved into his larger room with its tiled balcony overlooking the sea. During this trip, Ginsberg acted as the next in the series of midwives who helped Burroughs assemble and edit the manuscript for *Naked Lunch*.

In the summer of 1961, Ginsberg and Orlovsky made another trip from America to visit Burroughs. They expected to find him in Paris, but it turned out William had already left for Tangier, and finally they and Gregory Corso caught up with him here. An awkward time ensued. Burroughs didn't seem to have much time for his old friends, and he did nothing to hide his dislike for Peter Orlovsky. Peter eventually became fed up with the situation and left by himself to explore the eastern Mediterranean. This was a serious breakup, and at the time Peter didn't know if he would ever see Allen again. Allen left Tangier about a month later and sailed for Athens, intent on finding Peter.

Ginsberg's last trip to Tangier came in 1993. He went purely for nostalgic purposes, something very rare for him; he was usually scheduled so tightly with readings and interviews that he had little time to indulge himself. However, this time he took advantage of his improved financial circumstances to stay at the most expensive hotel in town, the Minzah [**Rue de La Liberté**]. One afternoon he rented a room at the old Villa Muniria and just lay in the bed, remembering happier times with Peter Orlovsky and his other friends.

6. Alan Ansen. Another friend and frequent Burroughs visitor was Alan Ansen. He arrived in Tangier from his apartment in Venice in late April 1957, just missing Kerouac. Since he had worked as W.H. Auden's secretary in New York City during the 1940s, he had practical experience organizing manuscripts, and he too pitched in to help arrange the chapters of *Naked Lunch,* giving valuable editorial advice. When the group gathered again in Tangier in July 1961, Ansen made the trip once more to see his old friends. In 1963 Ansen visited Burroughs once more, setting a pattern for the two to get together either in Athens or Tangier every few years for the rest of their lives.

7. Gregory Corso. In June 1961, Gregory Corso joined the rest of the group in Tangier. On this particular trip, Corso, Ginsberg, and Orlovsky stayed in rooms at the Hotel Armor, just down the hill from Burroughs' room on the ground floor of the Villa Muniria. One afternoon, the group posed for pictures outside Burroughs' door in the garden. While the friends stayed at the Armor and gave the reclusive Burroughs his space, Corso wrote poetry and made small oil paintings of imaginary views of the city. When the time came to leave in August, Corso borrowed some money from Ginsberg, which he immediately lost in the casino. The following year he returned to visit Burroughs once again.

8. Timothy Leary. Just after Peter Orlovsky left Tangier at the end of July 1961, Timothy Leary arrived. He was scheduled to present a paper to the International Congress of Applied Psychology in Copenhagen in August, but while he was traveling he wanted to drop in to meet William Burroughs. Leary had heard about Burroughs through Ginsberg and knew of his interest in drugs, so he wanted to turn him on to the new hallucinogens that he had been experimenting with. The two liked each other upon first meeting, and they made plans for Burroughs to visit Leary at Harvard and take part in his research. Once Burroughs was in Cambridge later that year, however the two found that they had little in common. Burroughs ended up rejecting Leary's approach to drugs completely and began to consider him a charlatan.

9. Lawrence Ferlinghetti. In June 1963 Lawrence Ferlinghetti visited Tangier. He had published Paul Bowles' *One Hundred Camels In The Courtyard* the previous year, but had never met the man, and he hoped to interest Bowles in doing another book for City Lights. Bowles wasn't in Tangier at the time, as he was was staying a few miles down the coast in **Asilah**, and Lawrence traveled there to see him. At first Bowles thought that Ferlinghetti looked too square to be the renowned poet and publisher, and suspected him of being a narcotics agent. He denied a toke of hash to the very man who'd just published a collection of his stories about cannabis. Soon Lawrence convinced him of his identity. Ferlinghetti wrote of Tangier, "Fantastic world, strange city . . . overheard conversational mummeries in six languages, kif-pipes everywhere, veiled women making eyes & cruising the Medina & Casbah, the skin of sun, the vaccine of dreaming."

10. Philip Lamantia. Surrealist poet Philip Lamantia was another who made Tangier his home for a brief while. After a year of wandering through Spain, France, and Italy, Lamantia settled in Tangier in 1964 at the historic Hotel Continental [**36, rue Dar El Barud**], on the edge of the old Medina. During his stay here, he met frequently with Paul Bowles, with whom he smoked kif and studied music theory. He also copied a substantial number of Bowles's recordings of Berber music; Philip was known to always carry with him a dozen pieces of luggage, including a huge, reel-to-reel Grundig tape recorder for just such purposes.

11. Others. Many other Beat writers made trips to Tangier, either to see Burroughs or simply inspired by his descriptions of the place. They all enjoyed the relative freedom of the international quarter, where it seemed as if everything was permitted. That live-and-let-live attitude faded after Morocco became an independent nation in 1956, but for a while the writers were able to pursue their interests without much interference from the authorities. The poet **Ted Joans** visited Tangier and fell in love with northern Africa. He returned many times, often on his way to his apartment in Timbuktu.

William Burroughs Jr. came to live with his father in his house on Calle Larache for the last half of 1963. Billy had gotten into a lot of trouble at school in Florida, and William's mother, Billy's grandmother, found that she couldn't handle the boy any longer. William made a half-hearted attempt at fatherhood, but for the teenager, perhaps not surprisingly, living in Tangier amid the drugs and his father's unorthodox lifestyle didn't quite exert a correcting influence. He was returned to his grandmother in Florida after six months.

In 1965 **John Giorno** came to Tangier at the suggestion of his friend Brion Gysin. Brion introduced Giorno to Burroughs, and the two hit it off. In the 1970s when Burroughs moved to New York City, he found an apartment on the Bowery in Giorno's building.

MOROCCO

JAJOUKA

1. Brion Gysin. Many of the Tangier writers, including William Burroughs, Paul Bowles, and Brion Gysin, were interested in the Master Musicians of Jajouka. Legend had it that they still practiced the rites of the ancient god Pan. Mohamed Hamri introduced Brion Gysin to Jajouka music, and they took several trips together into the mountains of Morocco to listen to and record their songs. In the summer of 1968, Brion Gysin brought the Rolling Stones guitarist Brian Jones to Marrakech and then to Jajouka to hear them play. (Paul Bowles noted that they were "very much rolling [in money] and very stoned.") The recording they made, *Brian Jones Presents the Pipes of Pan at Joujouka*, was released in 1971, after Jones' death.

MARRAKECH

1. Paul Bowles and Allen Ginsberg. In July 1961, Paul Bowles invited Allen Ginsberg to travel with him to the ancient city of Marrakech, where he had an apartment

Paul Bowles making mint tea in Marrakech, 1961

Paul Bowles on his roof in Marrakech, 1961

with a balcony overlooking the main market square, the **Djemâa el Fna**. They were here for a week or so and visited Christopher Wanklyn, a friend who also had a place in town. On July 20, Ginsberg described the evening sky in his journal: "The roof of the house – lying on mats drinking tea with portable radio & stove & rug & air mattress & candle lamp – lying back after majoun & cigarettes & pipes uncounted – the stars forming huge geometrical patterns, meteorites, and a land of roofs all around, some lighted & some dark, all stretching & jutting flat in every direction, broken by silhouettes of Koutoubia Mosque and others." The scene inspired him to write his poem "Djemâa el Fna in Marrakech," which begins with the following description:

> The din-ringing of myriad goatskin water sellers
> in between the rubbing of the drums of the
>> pavement
> seen from the hotel terrace with circles of Breughel-
>> Crucifixion-entranced crowds
> Listening to the white-robed storyteller in a hoarse
>> voice spread his hands and babble —
> the inner circle of the ring all children bug-eyed
>> hands clasped on their knees —

2. William S. Burroughs. From time to time Burroughs also stayed in Marrakech, including a month's visit in 1967. He knew some of the people in town, like John Shepherd and Christopher Wanklyn, so he was able to socialize whenever he liked, which wasn't often. He did enjoy the extremely low cost of living here. Another friend, Bill Willis, was redecorating the John Paul Getty Jr. house, which Burroughs described as "a huge palace with four courtyards, three fountains, the lot, and other people looking around for houses here in this last outpost of license the entire jet set will drain down here but I wouldn't want one of these medina houses like they all have." He preferred his own low-maintenance, low-rent existence.

ALGERIA

ALGIERS

1. Timothy Leary. In the fall of 1970, Timothy Leary, who had recently escaped from a California prison, arrived in Algeria without either a visa or a place to stay. At that time, Algeria did not have diplomatic relations with the United States, so fugitives had hopes of being welcomed here and believed they would not be extradited. Leary phoned the Black Panthers, who had been accepted into the country with the status of a revolutionary organization. Leary met with some prominent Panthers in the house he had been given by the Algerian government in the El-Biar district, and later the same day he was taken to see Panther leader Eldridge Cleaver at his villa. For several months Leary lived in room 23 of the Hotel Méditerranée [**Elle d'Jamilla, La Nadiaque**] with his girlfriend Rosemary, but was more or less under house arrest by the Panthers. Tim, who loved the high life, found the conditions less than perfect. In fact he called Algiers

Ashok Sarkar and Timothy Leary

157

a "sad, bored, uptight town . . . a backwater retirement village far removed and basically irrelevant to what was happening in America." He moved into a very expensive apartment in the center of town, but his relationship with the Black Panther Party crumbled. Finally Leary made another escape, this time to Switzerland.

TUNISIA

TUNIS

1. Lawrence Ferlinghetti. On one of his European tours, Lawrence Ferlinghetti flew south and visited Tunis. Later, remembering the experience, he wrote a poem he titled "Tunisian Nostalgia," which was published in 1993.

> Bare white marble room
> in that white hotel
> on a high bluff
> over the sea
> in Carthage
> The huge French doors open
> on the too blue sea
> Flickered reflections of waves
> on the high ceiling
>
> . . .
>
> in that darkened room
> rented for a day long ago

EGYPT

CAIRO

1. Peter Orlovsky. In August 1961, Peter Orlovsky fled an uncomfortable situation with his friends in Tangier and left Allen Ginsberg behind, traveling alone through the eastern Mediterranean. He stopped in Cairo to stay for a few weeks, enjoying the people, the historic monuments, and the opium. While here he moved from hotel to hotel in order to experience different parts of the city. He went to see the Sphinx, climbed to the top of one of the pyramids, from which he sketched the city and the Nile River in his notebook, and spent a good deal of time exploring the archaeological museums. In the evenings he went to the United States Library, where he discovered Herman Melville's 1857 Cairo travel journals. The biggest mishap he had was when two kids stole his favorite Parker pen in **El Tahrir Square**. (The loss was remediable. "Got cheap tiny Arab fountain pen that writes very fine spider web line," he reported.)

MALI

TIMBUKTU

1. Ted Joans. No one besides Allen Ginsberg traveled the globe as much as the surrealist poet-artist Ted Joans. Joans explored Africa as deeply as Ginsberg explored Europe, and was drawn to Mali, Morocco, Senegal, Sierra Leone, Upper Volta, Nigeria, and Algeria, to name only a few of the countries he visited. By 1961 he had decided to set up housekeeping in Timbuktu. "There were only a few

Photo Courtesy of City Lights Archive

Ted Joans, 1994

French residents still there. I rented a house that Robin Maugham had lived in. He was the nephew of the famous writer Somerset Maugham. The big house was made of adobe (not mud!)," he wrote in one autobiographical statement. The house was at **22 111th Street [also known as Omore Street]**, near the Djinguereber Mosque, and he reportedly paid $25 a year in rent. In New York City Joans had been a friend of Jack Kerouac and Allen Ginsberg, but not many ever made the trip to visit him in what must have seemed like a remote outpost.

Ted Joans was often quoted as saying, "Jazz is my religion and surrealism is my point of view," and he wrote many poems that dealt with the experience of being a black man in America. He said that he received a good deal of his "teducation" while he was living in Timbuktu. In one interview Joans suggested that "Africa should start sending missionaries out into the world. The missionaries would teach people how to be cool." One poem written in Timbuktu that unites these cultural strands is "Happy 78 Hughes Blues," an homage for the seventy-eighth birthday of black poet Langston Hughes.

I shadow dance near dawn
Here in Upper Africa
Where I stand with your book
And inherited legacy

In his April 1962 poem "Afrique Accidentale," Joans describes a trip from Dakar to Timbuktu in detail. He ends as he drifts off to sleep the night before his arrival in the ancient city:

So now lay me down to sleep
to count black rhinos not white sheep
Timbukto, Timbucktoo, Timbucktwo
I do dig you!
Timbouctu, Timbuctu
Strange, mysterious, silent & surreal
like a Sudanese Chirico

SENEGAL

DAKAR

1. Allen Ginsberg. In 1947, after a stay with William Burroughs in East Texas, Allen Ginsberg shipped out with the Merchant Marine from Galveston. In September his ship docked in the Senegalese port of Dakar, the western-most point in Africa. While in port for a few days Allen hired a local to do his menial kitchen chores, which left him free to read and write. He penned a story that he called "The Monster of Dakar" and a series of poems that he titled the "Denver Doldrums." He also wrote many letters, and in some he described the city. "Sex is nowhere

Ginsberg in his sailor's cap as he looked on his trip to West Africa

in Dakar. I have a couple of local pimps rushing around looking for likely prospects for me," he said. Dakar had adobe huts, grass shacks, beggars, and plenty of cheap marijuana in the form of cigar-size bombers wrapped in newspaper, but Allen's real dream had been of an orgy with native boys. Alas, his expectations never materialized.

DJIBOUTI

DJIBOUTI

1. Allen Ginsberg and Peter Orlovsky. On their way to India on January 3, 1962, Allen Ginsberg and Peter Orlovsky docked in the port city of Djibouti, in the small East African country of the same name. Allen knew that Arthur Rimbaud had spent time in Djibouti and wanted to see if they could find traces of his life here. They discovered that he had actually lived in Tadjoura, a town on the other side of the Gulf of Tadjoura, and they didn't have enough time to go there. They did manage to wander "into huge empty paved square several blocks wide – on one corner a stubby squat thick white-coned Afric Mosque Minaret and large elevated courtyard, across the street a vegetable & fish market – rays, swordfish, crabs – the other end of the Place Arthur Rimbaud congregations in tea shops," Allen wrote in his journal. The large plaza is now called **Place Mahmoud-Harbi**, and the Great Mosque still stands here.

KENYA

MOMBASA

1. Allen Ginsberg and Peter Orlovsky. Sailing cheaply from Israel to India in 1962 proved to be a bigger challenge than Allen Ginsberg had expected. He and Peter Orlovsky made slow progress and had to wait for available ships in several ports along the way. The pair reached Mombasa on January 12, but found that the next boat to Bombay was not until February 6. While waiting, they had plenty of time to explore the city, which proved to be charming and inexpensive. They registered at the Hydro Hotel [**Digo and Langoni Roads**], an Indian hotel equipped with crucial mosquito netting, and they dined in cheap restaurants on local delicacies for a mere forty-five cents a dish. Since they had the better part of a month free, they decided to travel inland toward Nairobi to see some African wildlife and to have an experience of local life outside of the city. When they returned to Mombasa to catch their boat, they stayed at the Hydro again and Allen wrote a poem that begins with the description:

> Hydro hotel, granite floor,
> white sneakers, round table with
> hat knife grey typewriter paper
> plate ink book on India — noise
> from the kitchen radio & rapping pans . . .

NAIROBI

1. Allen Ginsberg and Peter Orlovsky. When Allen Ginsberg and Peter Orlovsky arrived in Nairobi in 1962, they immediately left their bags at the Vadrahmut Hotel and went to the headquarters of the Kanu political party looking in vain for information about African poets. At party headquarters they were ignored thanks to their unkempt, scruffy appearance, but while in the office they glimpsed a flyer inviting everyone to the wedding party of a local politician, Tom M'Boya. The notice wasn't intended as an open invitation, but they borrowed ties and went to the trustee's hall on **Juwanjee Street** anyway. They had a good time, but even with their new ties, they didn't quite fit in and they were eventually asked to leave.

The next afternoon they went to **Nairobi Stadium** for a huge Kanu party rally at which Jomo Kenyatta, the man who would soon become Kenya's first prime minister, spoke. Peter and Allen seemed to be the only white men in the vast audience of tens of thousands of Africans. Later they took a bus to see Mount Kilimanjaro but were foiled: it was hidden in the mist that day. They did, however, see Masai warriors drinking blood fresh from their cattle's necks, which helped to make up for the bad weather.

BOTSWANA

OKAVANGO DELTA

1. Gary Snyder. In April 1994, Gary Snyder took his two sons, Kai (who turned twenty-six during the trip) and Gen, on a vacation to Africa. They stopped in several places to hike and to explore natural wonders on the Okavango River, and in the spot where the river forms the world's largest inland delta, they found an ideal place to observe wildlife. Snyder wrote in his journal, "Truly some sort of 'peaceable kingdom' if you don't mind the predators bringing down their meals." Here he spent time with a scientist who was an expert on baboon behavior and went on several small safaris to study the plants and animals. One day was spent near the crumbling remains of the **Ngezumba Dam**, where they looked at the elephant range and explored the abandoned campsite at Nogatsaa.

SOUTH AFRICA

JOHANNESBURG

1. Sinclair Beiles. South African poet Sinclair Beiles, who was involved in creating early cut-ups with William S. Burroughs, was born and raised, and spent the later part of his life, in Johannesburg. He went to King Edward VII School [**44 St. Patrick Road, Houghton**] before going on to the University of the Witwatersrand [**1 Jan Smuts Avenue, Braamfontein**], both in Johannesburg. In the late 1950s and early 1960s he lived in Paris at the Beat Hotel and helped Burroughs arrange the material for the first edition of *Naked Lunch* while working as an editor for the Olympia Press. Along with Burroughs, Gysin, and Corso, Beiles wrote and arranged the poems that made up their 1960 cut-up collaboration *Minutes To Go*. After returning to Johannesburg, he became active in Gallery III, a group of writers and artists who lived in the area of Yeoville, and remained in Johannesburg until his death in November 2001. He is buried in Westpark Cemetery [**Montgomery Park, Randburg**].

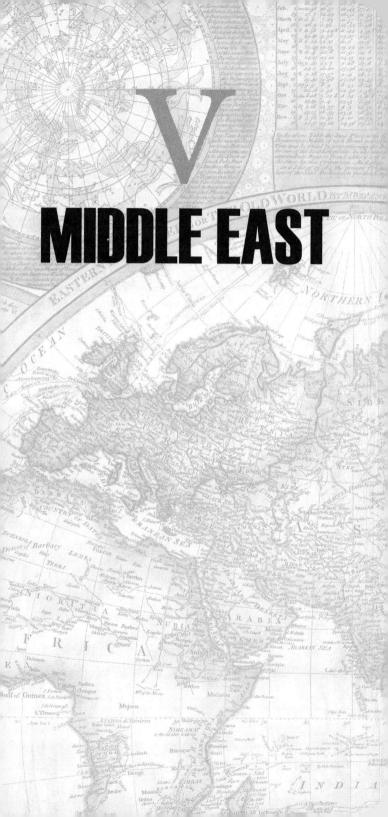

V

MIDDLE EAST

ISRAEL

JERUSALEM

1. Allen Ginsberg. On Allen Ginsberg's first trip to Jerusalem late in 1961, he paid a visit to philosopher Martin Buber, with whom he discussed drugs. Buber counseled Allen not to go seeking visions, because he believed they were only illusory and essentially unimportant. Allen was disappointed that he wasn't allowed to visit Old Jerusalem or the Wailing Wall, which were on the Islamic, Jordanian side of the border in those days. The trip was a political eye-opener for Allen. He felt that the Israelis had isolated themselves from what was going on in the rest of the world and he was surprised to discover that the Arabs in Israel were not treated well. He came to see the Arab/Israeli conflict as a problem that could not be solved until people were willing to forget their differences and identities—something that he thought neither the Jews nor the Arabs were capable of. Israel, he remarked, was filled with millions of people set in their ways, exactly like his own family, and whose stubbornness and blind loyalty would never permit them to compromise.

In 1988 Ginsberg revisited Jerusalem and read his poetry at the Jerusalem

Photo by Jasmine Stockett

Allen Ginsberg

Cinematheque [**11 Hebron Road**]. Steven Taylor, Allen's accompanist, flew over to provide music for the performances and they stayed together in a room that overlooked Gehenna, a ravine outside the walls. (Allen noted that Gehenna was synonymous with Hell.) This time Allen was allowed to visit the **Wailing Wall**, by then part of Israel, where he found himself weeping as he thought of the thousands of years of sorrows associated with that sacred place, ever since God had commanded Abraham to sacrifice his son Isaac on that spot. The tense political situation in Israel was palpable everywhere he went. He visited the Knesset [**Mishkan HaKnesset, Kiryat Hamemshala**] to talk with Palestinian moderates Mubarak Awad and Hanna Siniora before addressing a huge throng at a Peace Now rally.

Late one night Allen disappeared and didn't return to his hotel room. He remained missing for a few days, and Steven debated whether to report his disappearance. It turned out that Allen had sneaked across the border into Palestinian territory and spent several days with boys who made a living collecting spent Israeli ammunition for scrap metal. Allen found it sadly ironic when they showed him fragments of bombs made in America by the Bethlehem Steel company.

2. Janine Pommy Vega. Late in 1962, Janine Pommy and the Jewish-Peruvian artist Fernando Vega left New York for Jerusalem, where Fernando's sister Aurora lived. She helped them find a room on the edge of town overlooking the barbed-wire border at **Abu Tor**, south of the Old City. Before long Janine and Fernando married and settled into a relationship that allowed Janine plenty of time to write while Fernando made large pastel drawings. "Jerusalem was a walker's paradise," Janine remembered in her memoir, *Tracking The Serpent*. Wanting to explore Israel's border, she visited an old cemetery on the hill above the Hinnom Valley, watched by an Arab border guard who cocked his rifle as she approached. Janine and Fernando's marriage was not a success. (It was most successful, Janine wrote, on the sabbath, when there was nothing else to do but spend time in bed together.) Still, they stayed together in Paris after leaving Jerusalem. Within a few years Fernando was dead, leaving Janine a widow at the age of twenty-three.

3. Alan Ansen. In 1960 Alan Ansen took a short trip to Jerusalem as a guest of W.H. Auden and Chester Kallman. That trip became the focus of Kallman's poem "The Dome of the Rock," into which he incorporates Ansen's astute comments on the ancient city. They met the mayor of Jerusalem, and Alan remembered that he "loathed me, but I must confess I rather admire him." Ansen loved everything about the city and found it "a junction of joys I find too exquisite for analysis."

HAIFA

1. Allen Ginsberg. When he arrived in Israel from Greece in November 1961, Allen Ginsberg's first priority was to track down Peter Orlovsky. He hung around the American Express office in Haifa, hoping to get word from him. Allen made a few side trips to see some of the historic Biblical sites in Galilee, but mostly he stayed in town with people he knew. He tried to avoid the Israeli literary scene as much as possible and refrained from doing interviews and readings, preferring life as an anonymous traveler. Still, there were some people in Israel that he wanted to meet, such as Martin Buber and Gershom Sholem, a Kaballah scholar. He stayed in Haifa for a week before moving on to Tel Aviv, still hoping for news about Orlovsky.

In January 1988 Ginsberg returned to Haifa one last time to read at the University of Haifa [**Mount Carmel**] while he was teaching in Tel Aviv with the photographer Robert Frank.

TEL AVIV

1. Allen Ginsberg and Peter Orlovsky. It was mid-November 1961, before Allen Ginsberg and Peter Orlovsky were reunited in Tel Aviv, following their breakup that summer in Tangier. Even after combining their money they were nearly broke, and Israel turned out to be the most expensive place they had yet visited—worse, it was costly to leave, because they couldn't travel directly through any of the neighboring Arab countries. They stayed with a friend of Allen's, Ethel Broide, while getting their travel documents in order. Then, paperwork done, they relaxed and took some of the opium Allen had brought from Greece. From Broide's top-floor balcony they watched the orange-purple sunset on the horizon. Israel had become a friendly prison for them.

In spite of Ginsberg's outspoken criticism of Israel due to their treatment of the Palestinians, he was invited to visit Tel Aviv again in January 1988. He taught for three weeks with photographer Robert Frank at the Camera Obscura School of Art [**Rival 5**]. Allen offered a class he called "Photographic Poetics" and gave several readings around the country with his translator, Natan Zach. It was a perfect time to be with Robert, as Ginsberg was in the process of selecting the photographs that would appear in his first large collection of work to be published by the prestigious Twelvetrees Press, and he welcomed Robert's suggestions and advice.

ELAT

1. Allen Ginsberg and Peter Orlovsky. Once Allen Ginsberg reunited with Peter Orlovsky late in 1961, they tried to head for India, where they were expected to join Gary Snyder and Joanne Kyger. To do so, they made their way to the Israeli port of Elat on the Gulf of Aqaba. Since none of the surrounding Arab countries would allow travelers to enter directly from Israel, they hoped to take a boat to Africa, and from there connect with another ship that would take them to Ceylon in time to catch up with Snyder and Kyger. On the way to Elat they stopped to float on the salty waters of the Dead Sea, as all tourists must, and they visited Sodom after a long bus ride through the wilderness of Moses.

LEBANON

BEIRUT

1. Peter Orlovsky. In the fall of 1961, while Peter Orlovsky was traveling through the eastern Mediterranean alone, he stopped in Beirut for a few weeks while waiting for his next VA check. He found a room "overlooking vast view of sea, rocks shore and slope-hill buildings," but it had no electricity, so he used candles to read Hawthorne's "Young Goodman Brown." The landlord didn't charge him any rent since Peter was willing to clean out the trash-filled room in exchange. When he finished that chore, Peter moved to the YMCA. While in Beirut he met a few Lebanese poets, but he didn't like many of them. "[Most of them] work on newspapers and seem to love easy life. Some very involved with politics of Arab nationalism unity," he wrote to his mother. "They said Beirut big center for literary movement. Very little of their poetry translated except maybe for French. Saw but one poem by Yusuf-Al-Khal about wheat and food to grow—dull plea for better life for poor." Orlovsky was also cheated out of twenty dollars trying to buy heroin, and this disenchanted him with the city. Even though he felt Beirut was "sex-starved" in general, he did manage to meet a girl here and spent a good deal of time with her. When his money finally arrived, he headed on without her.

VI

ASIA

INDIA

Gregory Corso and William S. Burroughs both dreamed of visiting India, but never made it. Allen Ginsberg and Peter Orlovsky made up for it by spending nearly two years here. They traveled with Gary Snyder and Joanne Kyger, paving the way for other Beat writers such as Harold Norse, John Giorno, and Anne Waldman to follow. India became a source of spiritual inspiration for many of them, and their journeys prompted a new generation of Americans to explore spiritual paths via Eastern philosophies. Ginsberg initially went to India out of mere curiosity, in search of some peace and quiet, but it turned out that the experience completely altered his life and work. The ancient traditions practiced here, including a widespread respect for holy men and the ceremonial use of drugs, appealed to most of the visitors to India and became a part of the cultural fabric they wove upon their return to America.

BOMBAY [MUMBAI]

1. Robert Creeley. The first of the Beat writers to visit India, Robert Creeley arrived in Bombay by ship in January 1945. He did so not as an independent traveler, but as a member of the American Field Service during World War II. He drove an ambulance for the army and was stationed in Bombay before being assigned to Burma. While in Bombay he was billeted in Green's Hotel [**demolished, now the site of the Taj Mahal Hotel's tower**] and somehow managed to break his glass eye during this period. It proved difficult to replace in war-time India.

Peter Orlovsky, Allen Ginsberg, Gary Snyder, Joanne Kyger in India

2. Allen Ginsberg, Peter Orlovsky, Gary Snyder, and Joanne Kyger. In February 1962, Allen Ginsberg and Peter Orlovsky finally arrived in India from Israel after a long, circuitous journey and stepped off the boat in Bombay. It had taken them nearly two months to get here due to red tape, slow boats, and the poets' own very limited funds. Originally, they planned to meet Gary Snyder and Joanne Kyger in Ceylon, but because of the delays they had to revise their travel plans. They spent only a day or two in Bombay before rushing to the beautiful Victorian train station on their way to Delhi to catch up with Gary and Joanne, who were about to leave for the Himalayas.

All four of the writers returned to the city in April and stayed with an acquaintance of Allen's, Pupul Jayakar, at her comfortable home on the affluent Malabar Hill [**31 Dongersy Road**]. After traveling for three months in some remote parts of India they all enjoyed having hot water for bathing and clean sheets at night. On April 21, Snyder and Kyger left Bombay to return to Japan, and Allen and Peter stayed on for another month with the Jayakars. The respite gave Ginsberg a chance to catch up on a pile of correspondence, while Orlovsky fell in love

with Pupul Jayakar's daughter Radhika and dreamed of
having an affair with her. From Bombay, Allen and Peter
took a fifty-two-hour train trip to Calcutta on the opposite side of the subcontinent.

ELLORA

**1. Allen Ginsberg, Peter Orlovsky, Gary Snyder, and
Joanne Kyger.** On April 8, 1962, Ginsberg, Orlovsky,
Snyder, and Kyger took a guided tour of the ancient sacred
caves. Joanne found it exhausting to be dragged "through
the Buddhist, Brahmin and Jain temples" without respite.
She found the caves to be "unrelentingly religious, puri-
tanical and heavy," but it did inspire her to write a poem
in her journal:

> Come down
> Then chipmunk approaches
> & then runs away. Rats under the toilet pans
> at Ellora
> The flower
> fort.
> Now this path . . .

NEW DELHI

**1. Allen Ginsberg, Peter Orlovsky, Gary Snyder, and
Joanne Kyger.** On February 23, 1962, Allen Ginsberg
and Peter Orlovsky arrived in New Delhi on a morning
train from Bombay, hoping to connect with Gary Snyder
and Joanne Kyger, who had been in India for two months
by then. In Delhi Ginsberg and Orlovsky stayed at the Jain
Rest House [**Makhan Chowk**], a dormitory-style building
set aside for pilgrims and travelers, near the Jain Temple
in the middle of the old city. Travelers and pilgrims alike

could stay as long as they wanted, and it was practically free, with cheap, simple food included. During their two months alone, Gary and Joanne had already covered a good deal of northern India, making whirlwind visits to many holy places. Now in Delhi they were staying at a Hindu version of a YMCA just a few blocks away from Ginsberg's Jain Rest House. Allen left messages at the American Express office, and after a day or two the friends were united.

On February 24th, before finding Gary and Joanne, Allen went to hear one of the most renowned tabla players in India, Chatur Lall. Lall was playing at a farewell party in honor of a thirty-two-year-old disciple of Hindu spiritual leader Meher Baba. He was planning to take a vow of total silence. Baba had told the man, "Thru silence the first meeting between man and the mystery of God is accomplished." Allen wrote about all this in his voluminous journals.

It is interesting that, as detailed as his notes were, Ginsberg often overlooked Joanne Kyger, and seemed to regard her only as Gary's wife, when he mentioned her at all. Thirty years later, Joanne wrote about Allen's blind spot for women in a poem she called "Poison Oak for Allen":

> Here I am reading about your trip to India again
> with Gary Snyder and Peter Orlovsky. Period.
> Who took cover picture of you three
> with smart Himalayan mountain backdrop
> The bear?

Allen wrote many letters while he was in Delhi, describing nearly everything he saw and did. "India has everything Mexico has, poverty and dead dogs. It has hoods like Morocco and Moslems and shrouds and Indians like worse Bolivias and garbages like Peru and bazaars like Hong Kong's and billions of people like nowhere I seen." He continued, "crowded streets full of barbers and street shoe repairmen and bicycle rickshaws and Sikhs in turbans and big happy cows everywhere stealing cabbages from pushcarts." As they were all about to leave Delhi on March 27, 1962, they hap-

Joanne Kyger in the foothills of the Himalaya, 1962

pened to run into Gregory Corso's old girlfriend, Hope Savage, who had been traveling alone throughout Asia. Joanne wrote, "She comes with us to train, talking in high nervous southern accent, after Chinese dinner [at the Annapurna restaurant]."

HARDWAR

1. Joanne Kyger. On March 4, 1962, the traveling companions Ginsberg, Orlovsky, Snyder, and Kyger arrived in Hardwar to stay for a few days to witness the beginning of the holy festival Kumbha Mela, held only once every twelve years. Joanne Kyger gives a good picture of what travel life was like for her in her journals. "Reading *Kim* all day between bouts of laundry. A grey heavy wind dries the clothes on the porch. Lugging buckets from the faucets at the pumps. Soaking the clothes for 30 minutes in the room and back to rinse and bringing back a fresh bucket for new laundry soaking. Sleeping bag liners, shawl, Gary's parka, and on. Fruit salad when they return." Of course, the men avoided the mundane necessities of life and spent their time immersed in the religious activities going on. By contrast, Gary Snyder's journal of the same day reports: "Joanne wasn't feeling so well, so she stayed to rest at the Swarg Ashram while Allen, Peter, and I caught rowboats and buses to Hardwar."

2. Gary Snyder. As they arrived at the festival in Hardwar, Gary Snyder made these notes: "Busride to Hardwar through jungle and open acres of recently logged ground. Nomad camps with ponies under trees. Pass through a cholera checkpoint at the Satyanaraian Forest Guard Camp. Everyone without his paper gets a shot right there." He continues by describing the parade of holy men and saints, which he felt must have been going on in the same way for fifty thousand years. They stayed in Rishikesh and ate at the Pure Ghee restaurant, having enough left over to take with them.

ALMORA

1. Allen Ginsberg, Peter Orlovsky, Gary Snyder, and Joanne Kyger. On March 8, 1962, Ginsberg, Orlovsky, Snyder, and Kyger visited Almora. Their bus ride from Kuldani turned out to be rather harrowing. The road was so bumpy that many people became sick. "Sharp curves, shining white mountain tops," Joanne Kyger noted in her journal. Then at one point the bus stopped to pick up some people who had been injured in a jeep crash. Everyone helped gather their belongings which were strewn across the road, and Peter, who had been trained as a hospital attendant, administered first aid. In Almora, Gary visited a German guru named Lama Anagarika Govinda, a follower of the Kagyüpa Buddhist sect and the founder of the order of the Arya Maitreya Mandala. They all stayed in two rooms at a Dak bungalow for a few days. Snyder described Almora as a town in which the streets were narrow "and stone-cobbled, the house roofs are natural slate laid neatly on like shingles, and the wooden house-fronts occasionally well carved."

DHARAMSALA

1. Allen Ginsberg, Peter Orlovsky, Gary Snyder, and Joanne Kyger. At the end of March 1962, the four travel partners arrived in the town of Dharamsala, where the surrounding snow-covered mountain peaks rise to heights of 14,000 feet and forests abound. Here the Dalai Lama had set up his permanent headquarters in exile from Tibet. The first night, they ate at the **Lhasa Hotel**, enjoying "a meal of Tibetan noodles with meat in it," according to Snyder. It was their first non-vegetarian meal in weeks. That evening, to add to their decadence, Allen passed around his opium pipe and they all got high. The

Gary Snyder, Joanne Kyger, and Peter Orlovsky overlooking the Himalaya mountains, 1962

next night they stayed in a Triund Forest bungalow and hiked through the mountains for a couple of days before having an audience with the Dalai Lama. That meeting was to be one of the high points of Snyder's trip. He asked the Buddhist leader several questions about meditation techniques. Kyger asked about the practice of meditation in the West, and Ginsberg asked the Dalai Lama if he'd like to take LSD. He declined.

AGRA

1. Allen Ginsberg and Peter Orlovsky. On Christmas Day, 1962, Allen Ginsberg and Peter Orlovsky visited the **Taj Mahal**, said to be the most beautiful tomb in the world. Ginsberg had long dreamed of the day he would actually see it for himself. He and Peter posed for photographs in front of what Allen agreed was the most elegant of buildings, whose "glorious white dome hung in perfect balance in the blue sky." At that time, people were actually allowed to sleep on the floor inside the Taj Mahal itself at certain times of the year. Allen slept in his bedroll on the cold stone pavement and listened to men chanting and

Allen Ginsberg at the Taj Mahal, Agra, 1962

reciting Urdu poetry, which reverberated throughout the marble structure. With every letter he wrote he praised it, proclaiming the building "a giant Martian vibration eternity dome" and "the greatest human creation on the planet." Smoking plenty of ganja with the Urdu poets surely influenced these descriptions and increased the mystical power of his experience.

The pair spent a few weeks in the Agra area exploring the abandoned Mogul cities of Fathepur Sikri, Brindaban, and Mathura, the birthplace of Krishna. In **Brindaban**, an old woman named Shri Matakrishnaji, who was a saint in a Bhakti yoga (love-faith) cult, told Allen to start practicing Bhakti and to stop looking for a human guru. If he needed one, she advised, he should take the late-eighteenth-century poet William Blake, as his guru. Allen followed her advice and wrote, "Key of Blake I now think is acceptance of body, dismissal of all alternative universes and bliss in present love belly, rather than seeking spectral eternity."

BENARES [VARANASI]

1. Allen Ginsberg and Peter Orlovsky. In December 1962, Allen Ginsberg took a train to Benares on the banks of the Ganges River. Considered one of the holiest places in India, it is also thought to be one of the oldest continuously inhabited cities on earth. Peter Orlovsky joined him later, and they stayed until the following summer. The months they spent in Benares proved to be some of the most important in Ginsberg's life. At last he felt that he was completely cut off from Western culture, an isolation he welcomed. They rented a cheap room for nine dollars a month on the third floor of an apartment building at the top of the steps of the **Dasaswamedh Ghat**. Their windows overlooked the row of beggars who lined up in the street below to ask pilgrims for alms, and they were pestered by

Peter Orlovsky and Allen Ginsberg in Benares, 1962–63

thieving monkeys who invaded their room from the balcony. On his very first night in the city, Allen wandered along the Ganges and visited the **Manikarnika burning ghat**, where Indian families came to cremate their dead. Allen spent a good deal of his time watching their bodies burn on the funeral pyres. He learned how to chant with the sadhus who oversaw the cremations.

When Peter arrived from Calcutta they bought a few basic household supplies, like straw mats for the floor and clay pots for storing clean water, since they had no plumbing. They installed a 100-watt light bulb that dangled in the center of their room so they could read at night. Peter put his statue of the red-bellied elephant god Ganesh in one of the alcoves above the door along with his transistor radio and a few other possessions. They even bought a cook stove so that Allen could boil potatoes, and before long their humble pad began to feel like home.

Although he tried to maintain a low profile in India, Ginsberg did agree to give readings occasionally, and he lectured at the Benares Hindu University. At one point he was the guest of a Communist student group, but they were shocked to hear Allen's poems peppered with four-letter words, and it created a minor scandal. Meanwhile, Orlovsky struck up a romance with an Indian woman named Manjula. He also began to take singing lessons and learned to play the sarod, a traditional Indian musical instrument. Allen and Peter both took part in the giant peace rally held in Benares on March 8, 1963—the beginning of Ginsberg's life as an activist. They also took a wide variety of drugs, especially opium, which they found plentiful and inexpensive.

Once again, as it had in Morocco, the relationship between Peter and Allen deteriorated. Peter moved into a cheaper room by himself in an old cobblestone alley in **Bengali Tola**, a neighborhood farther away from the river and closer to his sarod teacher. For months the two rarely spoke. Orlovsky stayed behind when Ginsberg flew out of India, but within a year, the two were together again in New York.

ALLAHABAD

1. Allen Ginsberg and Peter Orlovsky. In late January 1963, Allen Ginsberg and Peter Orlovsky left Benares to see the *sadhu mela*, where 100,000 holy men gathered to bathe in the Yamuna River at the point where it joins the Ganges near Allahabad. The purpose was to cleanse and purify the river of all evil. The ritual bathing was an impressive display of Indian religious faith, and they stayed in town for three days, soaking in as much as they could.

Allen Ginsberg and the holy men, 1962

PATNA

1. Allen Ginsberg and the Hungry Generation. In April 1963, Allen Ginsberg took an express train to Patna, writing a poem about it called "Patna-Benares Express." In it he described himself in the third person:

> lost his identity cards in his wallet
> in the bald rickshaw by the Maidan in dry Patna
> Later stared hopeless waking from drunken sleep
> dry mouthed in the RR Station
> among sleeping shoeshine men in loincloth on the
> dirty concrete

While in Patna, Ginsberg met a young Indian poet named Malay Roy Choudhury and spent time with him and his family. Choudhury was living in Patna at the time, although he later moved to Calcutta. He was part of a group of Bengali poets who came to model themselves after the Beat Generation. They called themselves the Hungry Generation, and wrote poetry that challenged India's social and literary norms, rejecting the post-colonial values they believed were too restrictive. In addition to Choudhury, some of the more famous poets associated with the movement were Shakti Chattopadhyay, Samir Roychoudhury, and Debi Roy. Choudhury's use of street language eventually led to his 1965 imprisonment on charges of obscenity. Thanks to the connection made by Ginsberg, Lawrence Ferlinghetti published the work of many of these writers in the mid-sixties in his *City Lights Journal*.

CALCUTTA [KOLKATA]

1. Allen Ginsberg and Peter Orlovsky. In June 1962, Allen Ginsberg and Peter Orlovsky arrived in Calcutta

Peter Orlovsky on the Howrah Bridge, Calcutta, 1962

and set up housekeeping in a very cheap room on the top floor of the Hotel Amjadia [**Princep Street and Chandi Chowk**]. The hotel was so dirty that most of their new Indian friends found it too disgusting to visit. While in Calcutta, Allen met a man named Asoke Fakir, who presented himself as a holy man. Although the locals distrusted him, Allen was glad to have a native show him around the religious sites in town. Together they visited the **Nimtallah Ghats**, where the bodies of the dead are cremated and their ashes strewn into the Hooghly River, a tributary of the sacred Ganges. For six months Allen indulged his passion for both Indian spiritualism and ganja (cannabis). In fact, he and Asoke spent a good deal of time in a place called "Ganja Park" on the main road between Chowringhee and Rashbehari Avenue. The imposing **Howrah Bridge** connects the city of Calcutta with the western bank of the river and the train station. Its monumental steel design became an essential landmark in many of Ginsberg's works from this period, including "Under Howrah Bridge," which begins:

Black steel roof one mile long
Thundering to the opposite bank

near the bright blue / Wills Gold Flake
Bolt of light on Ganges
waters, and candlelight
in scows' rembrandt shadow . . .

While in Calcutta, Ginsberg made friends with many Indian writers around the university, including Sunil Ganguli, Shankar Chatterjee, Moti Nandy, and Shakti Chattergee. They often sat for hours in the International Coffee House, still near the campus and bookstalls today, enjoying hot tea and heated literary debates.

On his way home from India in May 1963, Ginsberg stopped for a few days in Calcutta at the Chowringee Hotel [**1, Jawahar Lal Nehru Road, Esplanade, Lenin Sarani, Dharmatala**] and wrote his poem "Last Night in Calcutta" as he waited for his flight. Orlovsky stayed in town in late July and August of that year with his girlfriend Manjula at **287 Jodhpur Park**. Then his visa expired and he was forced to leave India by train, crossing through Pakistan and the Middle East to Europe.

Ginsberg returned to Calcutta one more time in September 1971, staying for two weeks with his expenses paid by musician Keith Richards of the Rolling Stones. Allen was asked to report on the conditions in the refugee camps that had been set up for people escaping the fighting in Bangladesh dur-

Peter Orlovsky in front of Hotel Amjadia

ing the civil war. He and John Giorno visited the camps, where miserable conditions had been compounded by the monsoon rains. The heartbreaking experience prompted Allen to write one of his greatest poems, "September on Jessore Road." He described the suffering of the millions of people crammed into such a tiny space, and asked, "Where is America's Air Force of Light?"—a sharp criticism of the lack of humanitarian aid that could have been provided by his wealthy country, which meanwhile managed to go on "bombing North Laos all day and all night." Though immersed in refugee squalor each day, by night Allen was put up at the best hotel in town, the Oberoi Grand [**15, Jawaharlal Nehru Road, Taltala**].

GANGTOK

1. Allen Ginsberg. The city of Gangtok, to the north in Sikkim, was still a sovereign state when Allen Ginsberg went there (and it remained so until 1975). He had left Peter Orlovsky behind in Calcutta to straighten out his problems with the Veteran's Administration; in order to continue receiving his monthly checks from the Army, Peter had to take additional tests to prove his disability. In Gangtok Allen was given an audience with Gyalwa Karmapa, the spiritual head of the Karma Kagyu school of Tibetan Buddhism, on June 8, 1962. "He turned out to be a jolly fat guy like Jack Oakie who liked me and said he thought there was something definite he could teach if I could spend a week with him. So maybe in fall I go back," Allen reported in one letter to Paul Bowles. Allen needed an additional visa to enter Sikkim, but he had lost his identification papers and had trouble getting the travel documents. In the end he was allowed into Sikkim for a brief visit. "Walking in the mainstreet of Gangtok in rubber sandals after the town [had] gone to bed," he wrote in his journal. "Living in flophouse . . . Horses clopping outside in the rain, walking the streets alone. Immortal or deathless streets." In 1974, in his poem "Ego Confession," Ginsberg began:

> I want to be known as the most brilliant man in
>   America
> Introduced to Gyalwa Karmapa heir of the
>   Whispered Transmission Crazy Wisdom
>   Practice Lineage
> as the secret young wise man who visited him and
>   winked anonymously decade ago in Gangtok

NEPAL

KATHMANDU

1. Gary Snyder and Joanne Kyger. Before joining up with Allen Ginsberg in India, Gary Snyder and Joanne Kyger spent a few months traveling on their own. Late in 1961 they visited the mountains of Nepal. When they arrived in Kathmandu they found the cheapest hotel they could, called the **Himalaya Hotel**. Gary wrote in his journal, "It was so filthy and rat-infested that the next day we moved to a hotel a cut better." They spent a few days exploring the old pagodas, Buddhist stupas, and Hindu remnants. "Kathmandu looks rather medieval European, with narrow streets, two-storied brick houses with overhanging balconies, often carved wood decoration on the second-floor windows," wrote Snyder.

In the fall of 1995, Gary returned to Nepal, this time with his third wife, Carole Koda, and their daughter. They hiked up to a base camp on the slopes of Sagarmatha [*aka* Mount Everest]. Snyder wrote, "We went from Namche

Bazaar to Tengboche, then up the Khumbu drainage and from there crossed over an 18,000 foot pass to the Imja drainage up to the base of a mountain called Island Peak. We were with Sherpas all the way. Everybody was in pretty good shape and I only lost four pounds in a month."

2. Janine Pommy Vega. Hoping to find a culture that still had household altars dedicated to female deities and tended solely by women, Janine Pommy Vega flew to Kathmandu. She found a room in a small hotel near the Thamel markets, where she spent a good deal of her time. The monsoon season drenched the bazaar every day as she explored all the alleyways around **Dubwar Square**, the town's main plaza. "The oldest structures in the marketplace looked more like ornate temples than stores or houses," she wrote in her travel memoir *Tracking The Serpent.* "The door frames and windows were intricately carved with swirls and curlicues, animals, goddesses, and gods." From Kathmandu Janine hiked up into the mountains to take the Annapurna Circuit and get a view of the peaks in the distance from **Thorung La Pass**, 17,769 feet above sea level. At the end of her trip she wrote:

> At the end of the road
> there is no fair haven
> no hero's welcome
> no pot of tea
> at the end of the road
> is the road
>
> stretching in both directions
> in your heart.

BURMA

1. Robert Creeley. In 1945, Robert Creeley spent the final year of World War II in Asia, first in India and then in Burma. He moved around within the country driving an ambulance and working in the motor pool. According to his biographer, Ekbert Faas, "He was sent to Number One Company Headquarters in Sudanggi, Burma, then to Advance Headquarters at Monywa, and finally to a Jeep section in Shwebo, northwest of Mandalay." Creeley's platoon was then reassigned to Rangoon in May 1945. Recollections of his experiences in Burma crept into his poetry and later into letters he wrote to Charles Olson:

> on vines, stretched the distance . . . Three fucking
>   divisions waiting. Woosters, Gurkhas
> Sikhs, Queens own, & 7th, 5th, 11th. Waiting, for
>   them. On a road
> high sides, bullock carts passing all day, long. Real
>   tension. Then he comes
> the whole works, 1000 with him, . . .

Robert Creeley

ANGKOR WAT

1. Allen Ginsberg. Following his two-year stay in India, Ginsberg stopped off in Cambodia on his way to Japan in early June 1963. Here he became enchanted by the overgrown ruins of the temples at Angkor Wat, and composed a book-length poem in the course of a single night:

> Angkor — on top of the terrace
> in a stone nook in the rain
> Avalokitesvara faces everywhere   high in their
>   stoniness   in white rainmist
>
> Slithering hitherward paranoia
>   Banyans trailing
>   high muscled tree crawled
>   over the roof its big
>   long snaky toes spread
>   down the lintel's red
>   cradle-root
>   elephantine bigness . . .

VIETNAM

SAIGON

1. Allen Ginsberg. On May 31, 1963, Allen Ginsberg arrived in Saigon for a brief four-day visit. The capital city was just beginning to experience the U.S. military buildup that would soon grow into the all-consuming Vietnam War. Allen dropped in to the U.S. Embassy to talk to the U.S. Information Service officer of the State Department. In the course of their conversation they told Allen that the "U.S. regards the civil war as an internal issue," and that

"We will do everything possible to keep from being enmeshed in internal political infighting." Allen compared being in Saigon at that time to walking around "in a mescaline nightmare."

A few American newsmen were so bored waiting for something to happen that they concocted a story that ran in the *New York Times* under the headline "Buddhists Find a Beatnik 'Spy.'" They reported that Ginsberg, because of his unusual long-haired, bearded appearance, had been mistaken for a spy by the local Buddhists, who were locked in a bitter struggle against the U.S.-backed government of South Vietnam. None of it was true, but it made for a colorful story.

CHINA

BEIJING

1. Allen Ginsberg and Gary Snyder. On October 18, 1984, Allen Ginsberg arrived in Beijing with a delegation of American writers that included Susan Sontag, Toni Morrison, Maxine Hong Kingston, William Gass, Francine du Plessix Gray, Harrison Salisbury, and one of his oldest friends, Gary Snyder. The Writers' Union [**West Chang-An Street**] had invited them to take part in an exchange program that had already sent a similar group of Chinese writers to America. The American writers were scheduled tightly and constantly chaperoned. Allen, always hungry for experience, wanted time in China to just explore, so he asked the People's Republic to allow him to stay a few extra months to teach at the universities here, and they agreed to extend his trip through the end of the year.

Ginsberg found China to be "clean and safe and

vast and comfortable," as he wrote to his stepmother. He compared it to a "clean crowded India." As a group the American delegates went to many of the most famous tourist destinations, including the Forbidden City, the Imperial Palace, and the Chinese acrobat theater.

The many new small-scale, free enterprise ventures that were being introduced into China impressed the Americans, and Allen heard horror stories about the Cultural Revolution of the 1960s, which all the Chinese people he spoke with seemed to agree had been a nightmarish mistake. He reported that they were now looking forward to greater freedoms, though they maintained a commitment to a socialized economic system.

Francine du Plessix Gray, Masa Snyder, and Gary Snyder in China, 1984

Allen Ginsberg at the Great Wall, 1984

BAODING

1. Allen Ginsberg. During Allen Ginsberg's 1984 trip to China, he taught classes at several universities, including one in Baoding. Unfortunately he came down with a severe case of bronchitis and spent most of his time in bed, unable to get out and explore the city. In his classes at the university he found that his students were all "virginal innocent frightened eager boys and girls," encouraged to study English by the new modernization and Westernization policies of the very same government that had previously forbidden such study. Baoding was a provincial working-class town and represented the real China to Allen, far from the tourist circuit. Continuing his crash course on Chinese sexuality, he was shocked to learn that premarital relations were against the law. Although he was tempted to pose questions and make controversial public statements about homosexuality, he remembered his bad experiences in Cuba and Czechoslovakia during his 1965 trips and kept silent on these topics in public.

YANGTZE RIVER

1. Allen Ginsberg. On November 7, 1984, after the rest of the American literary delegation left for home from Beijing, Allen flew alone to Chungking. There he boarded a riverboat to take the famous three-day trip down the Yangtze to Wuhan. The lazy steamboat made its way slow-

ly through steep mountain gorges and navigated hairpin river bends, passing through the beautiful **Three Gorges** on the way. Even here in the countryside, the air was thick with pollution and soft coal smoke; Allen noted that all of China seemed to be covered in an eternal smog. He was escorted everywhere by kindly Chinese bureaucrats who took him to the proper tourist hotels and ordered his meals for him. Allen found himself envying a pair of bearded hippies he met

Allen Ginsberg on the Yangtze River, 1984

Photo © Allen Ginsberg LLC

who were traveling on their own in fourth class and eating nothing but tangerines and bananas. He missed the old days when he could travel anonymously without a chaperone.

SUCHOU

1. Allen Ginsberg and Gary Snyder. While Allen Ginsberg and Gary Snyder were still traveling together in China, they went to visit the Tang Gardens in Suchou. Snyder was delighted to be able to visit the actual site of Han Shan Temple, where the legendary Chinese poet was said to have been the abbot. Gary had translated many of Han Shan's poems, and on this trip he wrote a poem about how Han Shan's bell (famously located in the temple) resounded across the ocean all the way to California.

> The path to Han-shan's place is laughable,
> A path, but no sign of cart or horse.
> Converging gorges — hard to trace their twists
> Jumbled cliffs — unbelievably rugged.
> A thousand grasses bend with dew,

Gary Snyder in China, 1984

A hill of pines hums in the wind.
And now I've lost the shortcut home,
Body asking shadow, how do you keep up?

SHANGHAI

1. Allen Ginsberg. On December 2, 1984, Allen took an overnight sleeper train to Shanghai, only to arrive sick and miserable. He spent most of his first week in bed nursing a worsening case of bronchitis. Fortunately his official hosts gave him a big room in a hotel, replete with overstuffed armchairs and, the most welcome luxury of all, a space heater. When he began to feel better he went out on the narrow crowded city streets to explore the shops and markets. His teaching duties were light, but he enjoyed meeting the students, and he was careful not to cross the line of Chinese propriety when he spoke about sex or politics. From Shanghai Allen was able to take the train to Nanking on December 10 to see the Ming tombs and was happy to find that a handful of Zen monks were still allowed to practice here.

SOUTH KOREA

SEOUL

1. Allen Ginsberg. By 1990, one of the few countries left that Allen Ginsberg had not yet visited was South Korea. Late in August he finally got the chance, flying to Seoul to participate in the 12th World Congress of Poets. After it was over, though, he felt that the whole event had been a colossal waste of time. He compared it to meeting with a "million Poetry Society of America-type ladies who wrote boring poems." Ginsberg tried to call attention to the plight of some South Korean poets who had been jailed for political reasons. Although he managed to embarrass the government, his protests didn't lead to their release. The only rewarding aspect of the trip was getting to spend time with old friends who were in South Korea as well— Andrei Voznesensky and Bei Dao, an exiled Chinese poet—after which Ginsberg toured the country for a few days.

JAPAN

KYOTO

1. Gary Snyder. In May 1956, Gary Snyder arrived in Japan on the freighter *Arita Maru*, determined to pursue studies at the **Shokoku-ji** Zen temple in Kyoto under the tutelage of Miura Isshu Roshi. This was very unusual for a Westerner at the time. Gary would remain in Japan off and on for the next decade, studying Rinzai Zen, writing, and translating poetry from the Japanese. In the summers he went backpacking with friends, exploring the country's wilderness areas, and he climbed many mountains in the north during his first year here.

In 1959, after a pause to return to America, Snyder continued his studies under Oda Sesso Roshi at the **Daitoku-ji Monastery**. While he was here his first major collection of poems, *Riprap*, was published by Cid Corman's Origin Press, funded in part by City Lights. In February 1960 Joanne Kyger arrived, and once she and Gary were married they set up housekeeping together. When Allen Ginsberg came to Kyoto to visit them in the summer of 1963, they were living at **31 Nishinoyama-Cho, Omiya, Kita-Ku**. The following year Gary returned

Joanne Kyger and Gary Snyder in Kyoto, 1963

Gary Snyder in Japan, 1963

to California for a while, but went back to Japan in 1965, the same year he and Joanne were divorced.

In 1966 Philip Whalen came to stay with Snyder for a visit that extended over a few years. Kenneth Rexroth stopped for a brief visit that same year too. Following another trip to the United States late in 1966, Snyder moved back to Kyoto once more to study with Nakamura Sojun Roshi at the Daitoku-ji Monastery. In 1967 Gary remarried, this time to a Japanese woman named Masa Uehara, whom he had met in Osaka. The first of their two sons, Kai, was born in Kyoto in 1968.

2. Joanne Kyger. In February 1960 Joanne Kyger married Gary Snyder in a ceremony held in the U.S. Consulate in Kobe. She had long been interested in Buddhist studies and Eastern meditation, and decided to join Snyder at Kyoto's **Daitoku-ji** temple, but the couple was informed that it would be impossible for them to live together in Japan unmarried. The wedding was performed as soon as she arrived. Kyger began her own Buddhist practice in earnest, sitting for hours each day at Daitoku-ji's Honzan, but she was not allowed to sit in the

Joanne Kyger and Gary Snyder on dock at the Sea of Japan, 1963

main meditation hall, which was reserved for men. Joanne and Gary stayed together for five years, living in a small house at **31 Nishinoyama-Cho**. Kyger grew discouraged by her life in Japan, where her role as a woman and wife was expected to be subservient to that of her husband. She returned to California for good in 1964. During her time in Asia, Joanne kept a journal that was published later as *The Japan and Indian Journals, 1960–1964*. It is filled with glimpses into her life in Japan and includes many of her remarkable poems. "Cold | in the other room | the old lady | humming upstairs." Her witty and insightful thoughts are captured daily. One time Snyder asked her, "Don't you want to study Zen and lose your ego?" This shocked her. "What!" she immediately replied. "After all this struggle to attain one?"

3. Philip Whalen. Following Gary Snyder's example, Philip Whalen went to Kyoto to study Zen Buddhism in the late sixties on a grant provided by the American Academy of Arts and Letters. He supported himself by teaching English and pursued his Buddhist studies at the

Philip Whalen

same time. He continued to write poetry and prose, finishing a novel and numerous poems. His *Scenes of Life at the Capital* is typical of the work he did on his second trip to Japan, from March 1969 until June 1971. Portrayals of his life in Kyoto surface throughout it, from the dye vats along the Takano River, to the Kyoto Municipal Museum, to "paper lanterns floating in the River Oi | Souls returning to the flowery shore, | the Wind's Angelic Face | Puffing, happy . . ."

4. Allen Ginsberg. When Allen Ginsberg left India in 1963, he stopped in Kyoto to visit Gary Snyder and Joanne Kyger. That June he shared their small house at **31 Nishinoyama-Cho, Omiya, Kita-Ku** and spent long hours talking about Japan and Buddhism. Ginsberg was not yet a Buddhist, and it was during this visit that he attended his very first meditation session with Gary. A decade later, Ginsberg would take vows and become a practicing Buddhist himself. While he was in Japan, Snyder and Kyger took Ginsberg by train to see a scenic beach on the Sea of Japan before Allen left by train on July 18 to Tokyo, where he was to catch a flight to Vancouver, Canada. On the train he wrote an important and transformative poem called "The Change." As a result of all that he had learned in India and Japan, Ginsberg resolved to give up chasing visions via drugs.

NAGASAKI

1. Lawrence Ferlinghetti. On August 28, 1945, just a few weeks after the atomic bomb was dropped on Nagasaki, Lawrence Ferlinghetti visited the devastated city. At the time, he was serving in the U.S. Navy and had been assigned to Japan following the Allied victory in Europe. Curious about what they would find, he and several shipmates decided to view the total destruction caused by the bomb. They took a train to Nagasaki and walked through the scorched ruins where the city had once been. "You'd see hands sticking out of the mud . . . all kinds of broken teacups . . . hair sticking out of the road – a quagmire – people don't realize how total the destruction was," he later said. This experience was crucial in leading Ferlinghetti toward his pacifist philosophy.

KAGOSHIMA

1. Nanao Sakaki. In 1923 the Japanese poet Nanao Sakaki was born in Kagoshima, in southern Japan. He became a close friend of many of the Beat poets, especially Gary Snyder, Joanne Kyger, Michael McClure, and Allen Ginsberg. Like those poets, he was concerned about environmental issues, and many of his poems reflect the close relationship between man and nature. Sakaki's first collection of poems, *Bellyfulls*, was published in 1961 in a bilingual edition translated by Neale Hunter. When Snyder was introduced to the book, he looked up Sakaki because they seemed to share so many interests. In the sixties Sakaki became one of the founders of the ecological commune

Nanao Sakaki

and countercultural network "The Tribe." Over time he also translated the poetry of many of the Beats into Japanese, including Ginsberg's "Plutonian Ode." Sakaki was eighty-five when he died on December 21, 2009, in the mountains of Nagano prefecture.

SUWANOSE ISLAND [SUWANOSEJIMA]

1. Nanao Sakaki. Suwanosejima island, part of Japan's far southern Ryukyu archipelago, was the base for Nano Sakaki's communal group "The Tribe." Their activities were centered around the **Banyan Ashram**. The Tribe came to play an important role in the preservation of the coral reefs around Suwanosejima and other nearby islands. In 1988, when the Japanese government wanted to destroy the blue coral reef around the island of Ishigaki-jima by building an airport runway here, Sakaki organized a series of benefit readings around Japan that featured Anne Waldman, Allen Ginsberg, Gary Snyder, and Michael McClure, aimed at creating awareness about the destruction of the reef.

2. Gary Snyder. In the summer of 1967, Gary Snyder made his first trip to visit Nanao Sakaki at his Banyan Ashram on the island of Suwanose. It was here on August 6, that Snyder married his second wife, Masa Uehara, in a daybreak ceremony. Gary had met Masa a year earlier in Osaka, and with her he would have two sons, Kai and Gen. The couple divorced in 1989.

YOKOHAMA

1. Gary Snyder. In August 1957, Gary Snyder left Kyoto and shipped out as a seaman aboard the S.S. *Sappa Creek* from Yokohama harbor. He had found work as a wiper in the engine room, and he circled the globe in order to earn enough money to return to his Buddhist studies in Kyoto. He stopped at countless ports in the Persian Gulf, Italy, Turkey, Japan, Guam, Wake, Ceylon, and Hawaii. In February 1959, after being in the United States for nearly a year, Snyder was able to return to Japan on board the S.S. *Hiyeharu-Maru.* He returned to where he'd started out when the ship docked in Yokohama.

TOKYO

1. Gary Snyder. In 1998, Gary Snyder became the first American to receive the Transmission Award given by the Bukkyo Dendo Kyokai (Society for the Propagation of Buddhism), whose headquarters are at **3-14, Shiba, 4-chome, Minato-ku** in Tokyo. He used the opportunity afforded by the trip to travel around Japan once again.

2. Allen Ginsberg. The first of Allen Ginsberg's several trips to Tokyo was a visit to Gary Snyder and Joanne Kyger in Kyoto in 1963. Then in October 1988 he gave a series of benefit readings around Japan in support of environmental issues with Nanao Sakaki and Kazuko Shiraishi. At that time he was already in Japan for the opening of his photography ex-

Gary Snyder dressed in Japanese attire

hibit at the Watari Gallery in Tokyo. The Watari collection is now housed in the Watari Museum of Contemporary Art [**3-7-6 Jingumae, Shibuya-ku near the Gaienmae Station**], designed by architect Mario Botta.

VII

AUSTRALIA
AND
PACIFIC ISLANDS

AUSTRALIA

ADELAIDE

1. Lawrence Ferlinghetti and Allen Ginsberg. In March 1972 Lawrence Ferlinghetti and Allen Ginsberg were invited to participate in the Adelaide Festival of the Arts, one of Australia's biggest cultural events. The readings were crowded with large and enthusiastic audiences. During his reading at Adelaide's Town Hall, Allen invited four Aborigines onto the stage with him, and he used their song sticks while he chanted mantras. This was a faux pas in Australia's colonial society, where Aborigines were considered second-class citizens, and Allen's invitation created a minor controversy. Of course, Ginsberg was thrilled to have set off a scandal that highlighted the racism of white Australian culture.

MELBOURNE

1. Lawrence Ferlinghetti, Allen Ginsberg, and Andrei Voznesensky. In March 1972, poets Lawrence Ferlinghetti, Allen Ginsberg, and Andrei Voznesensky gave a reading together at Melbourne's Town Hall [**90/120 Swanston Street**]. Ginsberg had long considered Voznesensky to be the genius of Russian poetry, and he spent as much time with him as possible, both on and off stage. In

Andrei Voznesensky in Melbourne, 1972

Photo Courtesy of City Lights Archive

211

Melbourne an anti-Russian demonstration organized by some Hungarian refugees threatened to break up their reading. Ferlinghetti offered level-headed advice, telling Voznesensky to simply let the protestors make their noise, and after the Hungarians had spent all their energy, Andrei's reading continued without further incident.

MURRAY RIVER

1. Lawrence Ferlinghetti. While touring Australia, Lawrence Ferlinghetti took a week off between readings. He and his adolescent son Lorenzo headed for the Murray River, where they rented a houseboat and took a four-day cruise. "Last night on river, tie-up across from high white-yellow sandstone cliffs . . . Murray River burrowing down all those eons, Australia's Mississippi – but got no Mark Twain," Ferlinghetti wrote. (He did note that there was, however, a Tom Sawyer on this Mississippi, in the form of Lorenzo.) The two vacationers spent most of their time fishing from the deck of the houseboat.

AYERS ROCK

1. Allen Ginsberg. On March 23, 1972, while the sea-loving Lawrence Ferlinghetti and his son went off to explore the wild coastal landscapes of Australia, Allen Ginsberg went inland instead. He was drawn to the spiritual center of aboriginal Australia, the thousand-foot-high red rock formation known as Ayers Rock in English and as Uluru in the Pitjantjatjara language. Allen thought of this sacred mound as one of the wonders of the world. Ayers Rock sits in the middle of the flat plains of central Australia, in **Uluru-Kata Tjuta National Park**. In those days tourists were permitted to climb to the top of the rock, so of course Allen made his way up there, where he sat and meditated. He wrote a few postcards, took a picture of himself, and composed his "Ayers Rock / Uluru Song" using song sticks in the style of Aborigine song men.

ALICE SPRINGS

1. Gary Snyder and Nanao Sakaki. In the fall of 1981, Gary Snyder and Nanao Sakaki traveled to Australia on a six-week tour of aboriginal communities throughout the country. It was part of a program called "Poems of Land and Life," organized by the tracker and activist John Stokes in order to help create awareness of the plight of aboriginal peoples and the need to preserve their knowledge and way of life. Snyder and Sakaki met and talked in many places with members of the Pitjantjatjara and Pintubi tribes. Gary was impressed with the maturity of the young men, and he wrote, "Their religion is fairly intact, and most young men are still initiated at fourteen, even the ones who go to high school at Alice Springs. They leave the high school for a year and are taken into the bush to learn bush ways on foot, to master the lore of landscapes and plants and animals, and finally to undergo initiation."

FIJI

1. Allen Ginsberg and Lawrence Ferlinghetti. While on their way to give readings in Australia in March 1972, Allen Ginsberg and Lawrence Ferlinghetti took advantage of a layover in Fiji. Ferlinghetti's son Lorenzo was with them, getting a chance to play hooky from school in order to travel with his father. In **Koraleva** they saw a firewalk staged for tourists: after a kava-drinking ceremony, a group of men from Beqa island walked across

glowing coals and embers, seemingly with no effect on their feet. In the town of **Nadi**, Ferlinghetti was kept awake all night by the traffic noise, not quite fitting their preconceived notion of a quiet tropical paradise far removed from civilization. Ginsberg was inspired by everything he saw and wrote some songs, which he would later record. "Flying to Fiji," "Siratoka Beach Croon," and "Bus Ride Ballad Road to Suva" all were born from their few days here.

Allen Ginsberg, Lorenzo Ferlinghetti and Lawrence Ferlinghetti in Fiji, 1972

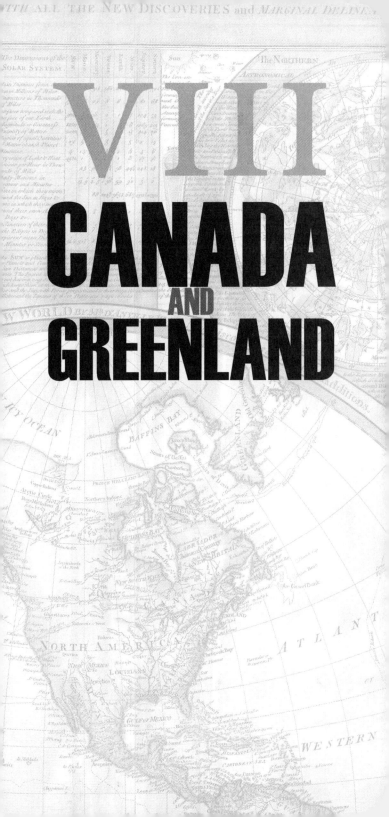

VIII

CANADA
AND
GREENLAND

GREENLAND

BLUIE WEST ONE AIRFIELD [NARSARSUAQ]

1. Jack Kerouac. In July 1942, Jack Kerouac worked as a scullion on the transport ship S.S. *Dorchester,* bound for the air base at Bluie West One. The airfield had just been built on the southern tip of Greenland as a refueling depot for the planes being sent to the war in Europe. Once the *Dorchester* docked, Kerouac and a shipmate went on shore without permission just for kicks and climbed to the top of one of the mountains that surround the base. Once on top of the 4,000-foot peak, they named it Mount Ford-Kerouac in their own honor. "And there we were, on top of the world, not 800 miles from the North Pole of the earth's axis, surveying our dominions of sea, land, and tremendously high free sky," Kerouac wrote in *Vanity of Duluoz.* It was fortunate that Kerouac did not sign up for the *Dorchester*'s next trip to Greenland, for it was sunk by a German U-boat torpedo on February 3, 1943, and 675 men lost their lives.

CANADA

SYDNEY, NOVA SCOTIA

1. Jack Kerouac. On Jack Kerouac's way back from Greenland aboard the S.S. *Dorchester,* the ship put into port at Sydney, Nova Scotia. Kerouac was not allowed to leave the ship, since he had technically gone AWOL on Greenland in order to climb a mountain. So he sneaked out, going AWOL once again to meet up with the rest

Jack Kerouac

of his shipmates and terrorize the town of Sydney. They spent the next two days drinking and visiting prostitutes, inebriating and exhausting themselves to the point where they broke into someone's house and fell asleep in the living room. He wrote of his adventure in *Vanity of Duluoz* mentioning that in the end he was docked a total of two days' pay for the escapade—$5.50.

CAPE BRETON ISLAND, NOVA SCOTIA

1. Allen Ginsberg. In August 1992, Allen Ginsberg flew to Nova Scotia to visit his friend and fellow Buddhist Philip Glass, who maintained a summer home here. They went on retreat at the Gampo Abbey monastery in Pleasant Bay [**1533 Pleasant Bay Road**], a Buddhist center established in 1983–84 by Chögyam Trungpa Rinpoche, Ginsberg's longtime meditation teacher. The monastery commands a beautiful view of the coast near Pleasant Bay, and the area was a popular one with some of Ginsberg's friends. The photographer Robert Frank also spent his summers in nearby Mabou Mines.

HALIFAX, NOVA SCOTIA

1. Allen Ginsberg and Chögyam Trungpa. In 1986, Chögyam Trungpa Rinpoche relocated the headquarters of his Vajradhatu to Halifax [**1084 Tower Road**]. Trungpa, the longtime meditation teacher of both Allen Ginsberg and Anne Waldman, was a major force in disseminat-

ing the practice of Tibetan
Buddhism throughout the
West. The poets had cho-
sen him as their meditation
teacher in the early 1970s
when he asked them to help
establish a poetics department at the Naropa Institute,
which he had founded in
Boulder, Colorado. On April

Chögyam Trungpa

4, 1987, a year after moving his headquarters, Trungpa
died of alcohol-related illness in Halifax. Over the years,
Ginsberg made many trips to Halifax, both before and
after Trungpa's residence. Allen read at **Dalhousie
University** and other venues, and in May 1995 he attended the Halifax enthronement of the Sakyong Mipham
Rinpoche, Trungpa's successor.

RIVIÈRE DU LOUP, QUEBEC

1. Jack Kerouac. In 1967, near the end of his short life,
Jack Kerouac set out on the spur of the moment, with a
friend from Lowell named Joe Chaput, to drive to the
town of Rivière du Loup, Quebec. Jack had developed a
keen interest in his family's genealogy, and they hoped to
be able to track down some traces of his French-Canadian
ancestors. It was believed that Kerouac's grandfather had
worked on a farm near this town, and Kerouac's father,
Leo-Alcide Kerouac, had been born in 1889 in a small
town just to the south named Saint-Hubert. Unfortunately,
Jack became depressed by the town's poverty and used
that as an excuse to begin drinking heavily. Soon the duo
left town, planning to do research in some of the larger
libraries in Montreal, but in the end they turned back at
the town of Lévy before doing any research at all.

KAMOURASKA, QUEBEC

1. Jack Kerouac. The first member of Jack Kerouac's family to arrive in the New World from France appears to have been Urbain-François Le Bihan or Urbain-François Le Bihan de Kervoac. Records indicate that he was married in the Canadian town of Kamouraska on October 22, 1732. When he died in 1736, his name was recorded as Maurice-Louis Alexandre Le Bris de Kerouack. Eventually Kerouac's grandfather, Jean-Baptiste Kirouac, would move from Canada to New Hampshire. All the variations in his name and its spelling, though, made it difficult for Kerouac to do a thorough genealogy by himself.

ST. PACÔME, QUEBEC

1. Gabrielle Levesque Kerouac. Jack Kerouac's mother, Gabrielle-Ange Levesque, was born in the small town of St. Pacôme on February 4, 1894. When she was four years old her family moved to the United States.

QUEBEC CITY, QUEBEC

1. Jack Kerouac Conference. One of the first international conferences to treat the writings of Jack Kerouac seriously took place in Quebec City in October 1987. The Rencontre Internationale Jack Kerouac was held over a four-day period in a former convent. Many of Kerouac's old friends, including Carolyn Cassady, Allen Ginsberg, Ann Charters, and Lawrence Ferlinghetti, made the trip to Quebec to speak before large audiences. Pierre Anctil, the director of the French Canada Studies Program at McGill University, collected the proceedings of the gathering into a book he titled *Un Homme Grand*.

MONTREAL, QUEBEC

1. Allen Ginsberg. Between 1969 and 1994, Allen Ginsberg made several trips to Montreal and read at many venues, including the Hillel House, Sir George Williams University, and Concordia University. In 1969 Allen stopped in to visit John Lennon and Yoko Ono while they were staging their famous "Bed-In" at the Queen Elizabeth Hotel, room 1742, [**900 René Lévesque Boulevard West**]. All the visitors sat on the bed and recorded "Give Peace a Chance" with John and Yoko. As Allen was leaving the city he was detained at the airport, though he was carrying nothing more dangerous than a few copies of the Canadian underground newspaper *Logos*. The U.S. customs officials held him for several hours while they inspected the contents of the paper at great length. The inspectors were unable to determine whether *Logos* was pornographic or not, so they sealed it to await closer inspection by the authorities at Kennedy Airport. This was not an isolated case. By the late sixties, Allen's name appeared on U.S. government watch lists of suspicious persons, and the authorities stopped and searched him at every opportunity.

TORONTO, ONTARIO

1. Allen Ginsberg. In addition to the usual readings he gave at various colleges around Toronto, Allen Ginsberg also came here to see a stage adaptation of his poem *Kaddish* in 1981. The play, which was sponsored by the Nephesh Theatre Company, premiered at the Theatre Passe Muraille [**16 Ryerson Avenue**]. It received good reviews and ran for several months. Allen thought the adaptation by Mordecai Greenberg was excellent, and he praised the production in a Toronto newspaper interview. "To end it with compassion, rather than horror, was good," Allen said.

VANCOUVER, BRITISH COLUMBIA

1. Vancouver Poetry Conference. In July 1963, Robert Creeley and Warren Tallman organized the three-week-long Vancouver Poetry Conference at the University of British Columbia. Creeley invited many of his friends to lecture and give readings, and even managed to bring Allen Ginsberg back from India for the occasion. Philip Whalen, Charles Olson, Robert Duncan, Denise Levertov, Drummond Hadley, Bobbie Louise Hawkins, and many others participated. Ginsberg, sporting long hair and a full beard for the first time, chanted the Hindu mantras he had learned from the holy men in India. He found

himself teaching his own version of free love, based on his experiences of the past two years. Writing to Peter Orlovsky, who had remained behind in India, he said, "I'm telling you the cold war's over, Hurrah! All we got to do is really love each other." The tone of the conference marked the beginning of a new era in poetics and heralded the social changes of the 1960s.

Charles Olson and Robert Creeley in Vancouver, 1963

2. Lawrence Ferlinghetti. Finding himself in Vancouver during one of the Apollo moon landings, Lawrence Ferlinghetti was moved to write a poem here that he called "Moon Shot." Later, in October 1977, he returned to Vancouver and the Pacific Northwest.

Participants in the Vancouver Poetry Conference, 1963

Selections from his diary notes and poems of that period, laden with images of the area's natural landscapes, were published in *Northwest Ecolog*. That month Ferlinghetti sailed on the ecological activist vessel *Greenpeace VII* from Seattle to Vancouver and wrote his poem "Written in the Greenpeace 'Dreambook,'" which begins:

> Dreamt of
> Moby Dick the Great White Whale
> cruising about
> with a flag flying
> with an inscription on it
> "I Am what is left of Wild Nature"

3. Ted Joans. On May 7, 2003, poet Ted Joans was found dead in his Vancouver apartment; apparently he had died on April 25 from complications of diabetes, but his body wasn't discovered for nearly two weeks. Before this, Joans had been living in Seattle with his companion, painter Laura Corsiglia, but he had grown increasingly disgusted with America's political situation. In 1999 an unarmed black man named Amadou Diallo was killed, shot forty-

Ted Joans and Lawrence Ferlinghetti at City Lights, 1999

one times by police in the Bronx, and when the police officers were acquitted of wrongdoing, Joans decided to move to Canada, vowing never to return to the United States. Not long before his death at age seventy-four he wrote, "So in my rather sorrowful impecunious state, I find myself filled to the beautiful brim with love and with this shared love I continue to live my poem-life."

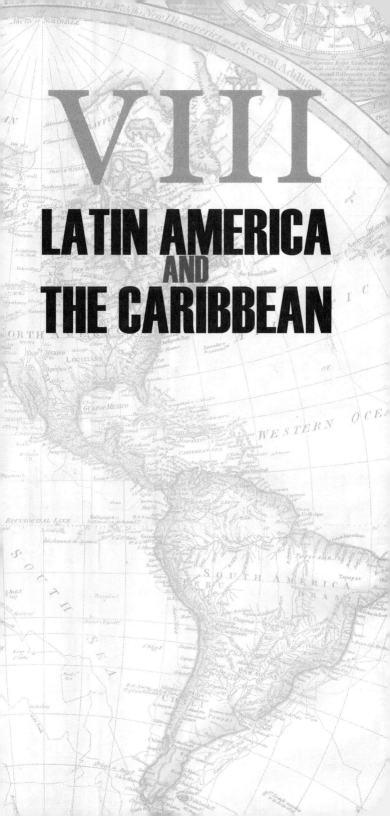

VIII

LATIN AMERICA
AND
THE CARIBBEAN

Mexico City

Mexico City, like Tangier and Paris, was the destination of many Beat sojourns. This was the Beats' city of choice in Latin America, and it was here that some of the more important events in their history happened. No other foreign city has meant more in the creation of the Beats' individual philosophies. Most of the members of the Beat Generation saw Mexico City as a nearby haven where they could rendezvous with friends, live cheaply, relax, write, and indulge in drugs without fear of the authorities. They were inspired by the lifestyle of the Mexican people, and the sights and sounds of Mexico found their way into their writings.

1. William S. Burroughs. Late in the summer of 1949, William Burroughs went to Mexico City to look for a house for his wife and children. He had grown tired of the problems he had in Texas and Louisiana and was searching for a place where he wouldn't be hassled about his drug habits. From all reports, William and Joan wouldn't have any problems with the easygoing Mexican authorities. In January 1950 he wrote to Kerouac, "We are living in a quiet, high class naborhood [sic]. Everybody minds his own business such as it is. I do not know what any of the nabors do, and vice versa. Down here curiosity is an unknown quality. People simply don't care what anyone else does. Even the landlady never asks questions." It was just the kind of place that Burroughs was looking for.

Initially Burroughs found a house to rent at **Paseo de la Reforma 210, Casa 8**, on the western edge of the city. Shortly after Joan and the two kids arrived on October 27, 1949, he rented another at **Cerrada de Medellín 37** (today known as **Calle José Alvarado**). The house was close to Mexico City College [**San Luis Potosí 154 at**

210-212 Orizaba Street today, Mexico City

Insurgentes], and Burroughs decided to pursue his studies here in anthropology using his benefits from the G.I. Bill. He started classes just after the first of the year in 1950.

From his home on Cerrada de Medellín, Burroughs corresponded with all his friends and invited them to visit. Kerouac came during the summer of 1950, and in August Lucien Carr and his girlfriend, Liz Lehrman, drove down from New York to stay with Burroughs for about a week. In addition to the family house, Burroughs also maintained a small bachelor pad for writing and private activities. The first of these was at **Rio Lerma 26**, and later he rented a room on the third floor of **Monterrey 122** for the same purpose. In early 1950 he began work on the book he called *Junk,* which would ultimately appear as *Junkie.* Later in the year he wrote chapters that would eventually become sections of the book *Queer.* While he was half-heartedly attending classes at Mexico City College in April 1951, Burroughs met twenty-one-year-old Lewis Marker in one of his classes and became infatuated with him, fictionalizing him in *Queer* as Allerton.

When classes were over in June 1951, William and

Joan Burroughs' grave, Mexico City

Joan moved to apartment number 8 at **Calle Orizaba 210**. They were living here when Allen Ginsberg and Lucien Carr drove down from New York City for a brief visit in Lucien's Chevrolet. The pair missed Burroughs entirely, though, because he was off on a trip with Marker, and so they had a reunion with Joan alone. The Orizaba apartment would continue to be Burroughs' address during dramatic times to come.

On September 6, 1951, William shot and killed Joan at a party in John Healy's apartment on the floor above the Bounty Bar at **Calle Monterrey 122**, near Calle Chihuahua, in Colonia Roma. Healy was the co-owner of the bar, and Burroughs had brought a gun with him to sell to someone at the party. He and Joan began joking about playing William Tell. Joan, who was drinking Oso Negro gin with lemonade, put the glass on her head, daring William to shoot it. He missed, and the bullet struck her in the forehead. On September 9, Joan was buried in a small unmarked grave in the American section of the Panteón Civil de Dolores [**Constituyentes, Miguel Hidalgo**]. In recent years her body was moved to a small crypt in the wall of the same cemetery, and a marker was added with her name [**Location Number 82, Class R, Section PR**].

Burroughs was arrested and spent about two weeks in jail. His lawyer, Bernabé Jurado (whose office was at **Calle Francisco I. Madero 17**), had him plead guilty to "criminal imprudence," and he was released on bail on September 21, 1951, scheduled to be sentenced a year later. In May 1952, while Burroughs was still awaiting the dispensation of his case, Jack Kerouac arrived for another visit and rented a room on the roof of the same building on Orizaba. Around that time, Burroughs moved to apartment number 5 in the rear of the ground floor. Here Jack looked over Burroughs' writings and suggested that he title his book *Queer*. A few months later, Kerouac returned to North Carolina with money he borrowed from Burroughs. In July 1952, Burroughs wrote to Allen Ginsberg about Kerouac, "I have never had a more inconsiderate and selfish guest under my roof. I certainly would not consider making any jungle expeditions with Jack." In the meantime, an old junkie friend, Bill Garver, had moved to Mexico City and rented a room in Burroughs' building. His young friend Lewis Marker also returned to Mexico City and stayed with William for a short visit.

By the fall, Burroughs had become discouraged both by the slow progress of his court case and by his own writing. Depressed, he wrote to Ginsberg saying that he was not cut out to be a writer. In November, just when things seemed like they couldn't get any worse, Burroughs' lawyer, Jurado, killed someone himself and fled the country. His professional legal advice to Burroughs was to do the same. In December 1952, when the Mexican authorities declared Burroughs a "pernicious foreigner," he knew it was time to leave. He hitched a ride with a man named Tex Riddle and left Mexico City, stopping first to visit his parents in Florida before making any future plans. In August 1953 Burroughs returned to Mexico City for the last time. His friend Marker was not to be found, and within a few weeks William left for good. On that trip he stopped at the cemetery to visit Joan's grave, but was unable to locate the unmarked plot.

Although Burroughs' books are not memoirs in the strict sense of the word, recollections of his life and travels creep into his works, and Mexico City figures prominently. For example, scenes like the following from *Naked Lunch*: "Day of the Dead: I got the chucks and ate my little Willy's sugar skull. He cried and I had to go out for another. Walked past the cocktail lounge where they blasted the Jai Alai bookie." In his next book, *Queer*, Burroughs describes Parque México with the oval Calle Amsterdam that encircles it.

2. Jack Kerouac and Neal Cassady. Mexico City was the destination for many of Jack Kerouac's trips. In *On the Road* he describes his first glimpse of the city "stretched out in its volcanic crater below and spewing city smokes and early dusklights." His first trip began in May 1950 when Jack was in Denver for a book signing. He, Ed White, and Neal Cassady decided to drive to Mexico the following month. Late in June they entered the city via Avenida de los Insurgentes and went straight down Paseo de la Reforma, gawking at everything along the way. Finally they pulled up to Burroughs' apartment at **Calle Orizaba 210-212**, the address that would be Jack's main haunt in Mexico City on this and subsequent trips. Jack found his own two-room apartment in the building, but Neal decided not to stay. What he was really after was a Mexican divorce dissolving his marriage to Carolyn, and as soon as he had the documents he left for New York in order to marry Diane Hansen, who was expecting his baby. On this trip Kerouac lived on inexpensive steaks, smoking marijuana and indulging in the teenage Mexican prostitutes on Órgano Street as often as he could. He went

Neal Cassady in photo booth

Photo © Allen Ginsberg LLC

to the bullfights at the Toreo de Cuatro Caminos, and the gore and cruelty he witnessed there was a factor in his decision to leave Mexico. Kerouac wrote about seeing his first bullfight in *Lonesome Traveler*. (Burroughs had exactly the opposite opinion of bullfighting. He wrote to Kerouac in one letter, "been seeing a lot of bull-fights. Good kicks. Going to a cock fight this evening. I like my spectacles brutal, bloody and degrading.") The bull ring was torn down in 2008.

In the spring of 1952, Jack Kerouac returned to Mexico City and the Orizaba apartment building for another visit. On this trip Neal Cassady dropped Jack off at the border town of Sonora, Arizona, and Jack took a bus to Mexico City. As soon as he crossed the border into Mexico, he experienced the same feeling of freedom that he had felt on his earlier trip. Jack had plans to write a character study of Burroughs, who was on bail at the time after having killed Joan, but he kept it secret from William. Amongst his adventures, Jack went up into the mountains with Burroughs, Burroughs' drug connection Dave Tercero, and Dave's girl, Esperanza Villanueva, for a huge fiesta. He also went to the Ballet Folklórico de Mexico in the **Palacio de Bellas Artes** next to the Alameda Central and frequented the neighborhood Turkish bath with Burroughs. While living on Orizaba, Jack wrote each afternoon and smoked a good deal of marijuana in Burroughs' bathroom. Here he composed most of *Doctor Sax*, considered to be one of his most experimental books. Near the end of his trip, Kerouac went to see the church of Santa María la Redonda, described in beautiful detail in *Lonesome Traveler*, including its "great tormented statue of Christ on the Cross." The next day, July 1, 1952, Jack borrowed $20 from Burroughs and left town. It was just enough to get him back to his sister's house in North Carolina, where he continued to work on *Doctor Sax*.

In December 1952, Burroughs had already left Mexico City by the time Jack Kerouac and Neal Cassady pulled into town again. The ever-restless Cassady stayed with Kerouac in Burroughs' old apartment on Orizaba for a few days, just long enough to score some marijuana, and then he was gone. Jack used a lot of benzedrine on this trip

Jack Kerouac, Allen Ginsberg, Peter Orlovsky, Gregory Corso, and Lafcadio Orlovsky in Mexico City, 1956

and wrote "Benzedrine Vision / Mexico Thieves Market / Memoirs of a Bebopper," the manuscripts of which are in the Kerouac archive at the New York Public Library today. Then he began another novel that would turn into *Maggie Cassidy* and visited with Bill Garver. "I took a little dobe block up on Bill's roof, 2 rooms, lots of sun and old Indian women doing the wash. Will stay here awhile even though $12 a month is high rent. But perfect place to write, blast, think, fresh air, sun, moon, stars, the Roof of the City. I even bought Mexican pottery to brighten my 2 cells." Around Christmas Jack hitchhiked back to the United States.

With a $200 grant from the National Academy of

Kerouac's rooftop shack in Mexico City

Arts and Letters in his pocket, Kerouac made his next trip to Mexico City in August 1955, heading south ostensibly to buy cheap penicillin for his phlebitis. He stayed with Bill Garver until renting his old adobe hut once again on the rooftop at **Calle Orizaba**. He tried to look up Dave Tercero, but found that he was dead. He then promptly fell in love with Tercero's widow, Esperanza, and their love affair became the subject of his book *Tristessa*. He spent a month in the city, writing many of the 150 choruses that would become *Mexico City Blues*. He boarded a bus to El Paso in early September with his pockets full of benzedrine and marijuana, eventually meeting up with Ginsberg and Gary Snyder in San Francisco, where he arrived just in time to sit in the audience and pass around the wine jug at the famous Six Gallery reading.

Later that same autumn, Kerouac decided to return to Mexico City. This time he caught a bus from Nogales, Arizona, to the Mexican capital, where the very same rooftop room on Orizaba was faithfully waiting for him to rent it again. It overlooked the "drear, even sad, darkness" of the city, he wrote. Here he stayed while writing *Desolation Angels, Tristessa*, and some additional choruses for *Mexico*

City Blues. After Ginsberg closed up his apartment in Berkeley and organized a trip to Mexico with Gregory Corso, and Peter and Lafcadio Orlovsky, they all appeared in Mexico City at the beginning of November 1956. With Jack they played tourists and visited the Floating Gardens of Lake Xochimilco and the Tenochtitlán pyramids. "I caught a cold | From the sun | When they tore my heart out | At the top of the pyramid" Jack wrote in *Mexico City Blues.* Kerouac also indulged his artistic impulse by painting murals on the walls of his adobe apartment and drawing pictures of his dead brother, Gerard, and some religious subjects. When the time came to leave, everyone except Corso hitched rides north.

In the summer of 1957, Kerouac was again looking for solitude in which to write. He believed that if he could escape to Mexico City once more, he could concentrate on his literary pursuits. At the end of July he left his mother's place in Orlando and headed for Mexico City, planning to stay for at least six weeks. When he arrived, he discovered that his friend Bill Garver had died in the old apartment on Orizaba. To make matters worse, the city was hit by a major earthquake on July 28 that killed sixty-eight people and destroyed or damaged hundreds of buildings. Fortunately, Jack, who was staying at the Hotel Luis Moya, was unhurt. In a letter he wrote that he was living in "an old 1910 whorehouse built of solid marble and tile and not one crack in our walls." However the city's infrastructure suffered tremendously, and the contaminated water supply probably contributed to an illness that forced Kerouac to return to his mother's house in Orlando in mid-August.

Kerouac's final trip to Mexico City was in June 1961, when he rented a room at **Cerrada de Medellín 13-A**, the same building in which William and Joan Burroughs had once lived. He described it as a "dismal dusty streetdoor apartment." It became the namesake of his "Cerrada

Medellín Blues." In the end he became disgusted with the city altogether when thieves broke into his room and took his clothes and sleeping bag, and he went home.

3. Allen Ginsberg. The first trip Allen Ginsberg made to Mexico City was with Lucien Carr in late August 1951, when the two decided at the last minute to attend the wedding of one of Carr's friends. When they stopped in to see William and Joan Burroughs on this spur-of-the-moment visit, William wasn't in town, but Joan showed them around. She also treated them to a wild, drunken car ride over the mountains to the west coast, while Ginsberg and Joan's two children held on for dear life in the backseat.

In May 1954, after spending several months in the isolated jungles of Chiapas, Ginsberg stopped in Mexico City for a few days on his way to California. He stayed at the Hotel Geneve [**Londres 130**], which had been recommended to him by friends. At the time it was a cheap place, plagued by bedbugs, but adequate for his needs. (Today it has been greatly improved and is quite luxurious.) Allen was too broke to prolong his stay even in the

Allen Ginsberg and Lucien Carr (near the top on the left) at Russ Lafferty's wedding in Mexico, 1951

most modest of hotels, and he'd hoped Bill Garver would put him up, but wasn't able to find him. Ginsberg was carrying letters of introduction from his college teacher Meyer Shapiro to the artists Rufino Tamayo and Miguel Covarrubias, as well as the Mexican poet laureate Carlos Pellicer, but these were people to meet for coffee, not to ask for a couch to sleep on. Running out of money fast, he was forced to move on.

In November 1956, Ginsberg returned to the city with Jack Kerouac, Gregory Corso, and Peter and Lafcadio Orlovsky. This time he stayed for two weeks, leading his friends around to the major tourist sites and museums. They were drunk and high so much of the time that even Allen became exhausted and eventually wrote, "I can't stand it anymore." They went out to see the **Pyramid of the Sun** at Teotihuacán, sitting on the peak of the monument staring at the sky with the vast shining valley of Mexico stretched out below, and eventually retreating from the sun into the network of cooler

Lucien Carr and Allen Ginsberg having cocktails

caves underneath the pyramids. They visited the floating gardens at Xochimilco and went to the national ballet in the Palacio de Bellas Artes where they sat in the upper balcony for thirty-four cents each. They even stopped to pose in the public garden for a souvenir group portrait that later became an iconic Beat photo (see page 233). On several occasions they visited the **Calle del Órgano**, one of the red light districts of Mexico City. Peter contracted gonorrhea, which he passed along to Allen, but the more prudent Kerouac used protection and didn't contract any diseases. In his journal Allen painted a word picture of their trip: "walked late at night down grand streets all lit up full of tortilla and sweater stands and cheesy mex burlesque and comedian theatres, ate big steaks cheap at expensive restaurant, listened to Gregory recite incessantly, he was always spontaneously scribbling in big 10-cent notebook, Peter talked to children, Lafcadio dawdled behind us on the street, I met the fairies and had big orgies." Allen, always honest, quickly revised the last phrase to say "little orgies," and then crossed that out to say "not much of one really."

Ten years later in 1965, on his way to visit Cuba, Ginsberg passed through Mexico City once more. He stayed with Margaret Randall, the editor of the bilingual literary magazine *El Corno Emplumado*. Allen had been looking forward to the trip, hoping to revisit some of the haunts he had frequented with Burroughs and Kerouac, but he collapsed in bed with the grippe. He barely moved for three days, although he noticed everything there was to take in from his sickbed. In a letter he wrote, "Mexico City still had that beautiful funky smell of Mex Tabac and detritus and tropic earth perfume." At night the same green lamps lit the Alameda Central, but he couldn't get out to enjoy it on this visit.

By August 1981, when Ginsberg next returned to Mexico City, he was one of the most famous writers in the world. That year he was invited to attend the Mexico City International Poetry Conference along with Andrei Voznesensky, Jorge Luis Borges, Günter Grass, W.S. Merwin, and Octavio Paz. Ginsberg stayed with the other conference notables at the luxurious Chapultepec Presidente Hotel [**Campos Eliseos 218**], but he felt hypocritical living amidst such wealth in a land of poverty.

4. Gregory Corso. The fall 1956 trip with Ginsberg, Kerouac, and the Orlovskys was Gregory Corso's first encounter with Mexico. He wasn't at all impressed. He thought the place was dirty and dangerous, although he did enjoy the spectacular Aztec ruins and artifacts. At the pyramids of Teotihuacán he traded his favorite Harvard belt for the souvenirs that the little Indian boys were hawking, proud of his bargaining ability. When the other four caught a ride back north, Corso decided to wait for some promised travel money so that he could fly home in style, but the place where they had been staying on Orizaba Street was "too grubby" for him, and he moved to a much better hotel. "Mexico is poor, sick, and nowhere," he confided to Lawrence Ferlinghetti in a letter. While waiting for his plane fare, which took almost a month to arrive, he wrote many of the poems that were to appear in his collection *Gasoline*. One short poem he used as part of the series "Mexican Impressions" describes his visit to the city's zoo and became one of his favorites:

> In the Mexican Zoo
> they have ordinary
> American cows.

5. Lawrence Ferlinghetti. Perhaps the first Beat writer to visit Mexico City was Lawrence Ferlinghetti. While he was still an undergraduate at the University of North Carolina in 1939, he and two friends took a summer trip

Homero Aridjis, unknown, Lars Forrsell, and Lawrence Ferlinghetti at Trotsky's house in Mexico City, 1982

to Mexico. They chose Mexico because one of the boys was the nephew of Josephus Daniels, a former Secretary of the Navy who was then serving as the U.S. Ambassador to Mexico under President Roosevelt. Lawrence's travel buddy was certain they could stay with his uncle, but when they got to Mexico City the ambassador proffered no invitation, so they ended up in a cheap pension. Ferlinghetti wrote stories about the Mexican political system and sent them off to *Time* magazine, hoping they would publish them. They did not.

Lawrence returned to Mexico City numerous times over the years. In his book *The Mexican Night* he describes a visit he made in September 1968, when the Mexican government was gearing up to host the Olympics and student protests gripped the country. "I go to the occupied University of Mexico campus in late afternoon – with some poets and editors of *El Corno Emplumado* – and pass through the barricades into the buildings held by the students, like Cuba 1960 with young cats in fatigues guarding the entrances & chicks with rifles. A calm prevails today. In the Med School the students have embalmed the bodies of some of their comrades killed by the government of the people." This unrest would culminate tragically in October with the Tlatelolco massacre, in which uncounted numbers of students were killed.

Ferlinghetti also attended the Second International Poetry Festival of Morelia here in 1982. The geographical inconsistency is no mistake: the site of the festival had been moved at the last minute from Morelia, the capital of Michoacán, to Mexico City. As Ferlinghetti remarked in his journals, "about 1/3 of the invited came, after being informed of the shift from beautiful Morelia to this monster sprawling metropolis of traffic, dust, torn up streets, millions of poor people like rats or ants in a hive." Organized by Mexican poet Homero Aridjis, the festival also included Ted Hughes and Octavio Paz.

6. Philip Lamantia. The surrealist poet Philip Lamantia spent a great deal of time in Mexico during his youthful years, often feeding his intense interest in mysticism. Philip first traveled to the country in 1950, inspired by Antonin Artaud's *Voyage to the Land of the Tarahumara*. He hoped to participate in a peyote ritual, in the wake of a visionary experience he'd had at a peyote rite with the Washoe Indians of the California Sierra. While this particular quest proved fruitless, he fell in love with Mexico and vowed to return.

In 1954, Lamantia moved with photographer Goldian Nesbit to Mexico City, where they rented a house on **Calle Zacatecas** near the university. The house served as headquarters for explorations of the city and environs. In his pursuit of Mexican surrealism and surrealists, Philip met and befriended the painter Leonora Carrington and others in her circle.

In 1959 Lamantia lived with Lucille Dejardin, a French theatrical costume designer, in a Mexico City flat at **Oslo 3** in the Zona Rosa; they later moved to an apartment on **Calle de Río Hudson**. In this period, he became friends with Mexican poet Homero Aridjis, Nicaraguan poet-priest Ernesto Cardenal, and Sergio Mondragón, through whom he met other writers and artists in the *Corno Emplumado* circle. In 1961, Philip and Lucille were married in the church of Santa María in the small village of Ahuacatitlán in Morelos.

Late one dark night in 1961, Lamantia and a painter friend named Aymon de Sales climbed up the **Pyramid of the Sun** at Teotihuacán, just outside Mexico City. His poem "The Pyramid Scene" invokes the terrifying apparitions that menaced the two of them. In 1962, the year after his book *Destroyed Works* was published, Philip was deported from Mexico due to his association with a suspected drug dealer, and both his times in Mexico and his marriage came to an end.

7. Lucien Carr and David Kammerer. In 1940, a Boy Scout leader named David Kammerer brought a fourteen-year-old scout named Lucien Carr with him on a brief trip to Mexico City, with the approval of Carr's mother. This was the beginning of a lifelong obsession for Kammerer. He followed Carr around the U.S. for several years until 1944, when Carr stabbed him to death one night in New York City. Carr returned to Mexico several times over the years, some of which have been described earlier.

8. Ray and Bonnie Bremser. Writers Ray and Bonnie Bremser spent a good deal of time in Mexico City, often trying to clear up legal and immigration problems at various government offices. On most trips to the city, Bonnie turned tricks to earn enough money to finance their wandering. The city appears in Bonnie's memoir, *Troia*, and in many of Ray's poems. After the hard-luck couple gave their daughter, Rachel, up for adoption, they arrived in Mexico City haunted by nightmares and hallucinations. The first night they stayed in a "much-too-extravagant 100 peso room

Ray Bremser

in the Hotel Majestic on the plaza of the Zócalo," Bonnie remembered. The plaza reminded her of Red Square. She reports that they hid out here before moving to a cheaper hotel in **Villa de Guadalupe**, on the northern outskirts of town, all the while imagining that they were being watched by the police and the F.B.I. During their many visits, they seldom seemed to stay in the same place twice. Once they found a hotel a block from Avenida Juárez and the **Palacio de Bellas Artes**, where Bonnie admired the Siqueiros paintings. It wasn't a very good neighborhood, she said, filled with "low life, milling no-goods of the streets – mostly men, pimps, and vagrant types." Ray liked to spend time in the nearby **Alameda Central**, scoring drugs and writing poems. On another occasion, probably in 1961, they stayed with Philip Lamantia.

9. El Corno Emplumado. One of the first periodicals to appear in Latin America that focused on the Beat Generation was *El Corno Emplumado*, a magazine edited by Margaret Randall and Sergio Mondragón. This bilingual publication featured the work of Ginsberg, Ferlinghetti, Creeley, Snyder, and many others, from 1962 through 1969. Due to political pressure the magazine was forced to close after the 1968 student movement. A more detailed account of the government's harassment tactics is described in a letter written by Randall and reproduced in the original edition of Lawrence Ferlinghetti's *The Mexican Night*.

MEXICO

Mexico proved to be the destination of choice for many members of the Beat Generation, almost becoming an aesthetic rite of passage for each of them. The country had the advantages of being inexpensive, convenient to get to, generous in its reception of foreigners, tolerant in its drug laws, sexually permissive, and eternally exotic. Several writers lived here for long periods of time while others made only periodic visits, but all of them described their experiences in their poetry, prose, and correspondence.

BAJA CALIFORNIA

1. Lawrence Ferlinghetti. The peninsula of Baja California is just over the border from San Diego County, and so it proved a convenient retreat from both Los Angeles and San Francisco. Lawrence Ferlinghetti loved to vacation in Baja, and more than once drove down the coast to San Felipe on the Sea of Cortez. Ferlinghetti found the area relaxing and its landscapes inspirational.

In "Baja Revisited" he writes of the pristine, unspoiled nature of the area:

> Baja wild baja
> still a last frontier
> here on the left side of the world
> still nothing but sand sand sand
> deserts and mountains and wild ocean
> cacti gesturing against the sky
> by the Sea of Cortez . . .

And in another poem from the same era, "Baja Beatitudes," he depicts two fishermen he encountered at **Playa Requesón**, on the Bahía de Concepción near Mulegé:

> and the two old fishermen
> ancient of days
> grizzled brothers grown to old age
> on this far beach
>   *hermanos in soledad*
> the older of the two
> bent and bearded
> singing to the gulls
> in a high crazy voice. . . .

TIJUANA [BAJA CALIFORNIA NORTE]

1. Lawrence Ferlinghetti. In *The Mexican Night,* Lawrence Ferlinghetti writes about his first trips to Mexico via Tijuana, just across the border from San Diego. On one of the trips he traveled with two friends from La Jolla, and he wrote, "Digging the jumbled streets, eating roast corn from street-vendors, drinking Cerveza under arbors in back gardens of crazy hillside restaurants." On the way back through Tijuana, he noted a legless "public writer" in the street, operating from the back of a broken car with a typewriter, taking dictations from passersby who needed documents typed.

ENSENADA [BAJA CALIFORNIA NORTE]

1. Lawrence Ferlinghetti. In October 1961, Lawrence Ferlinghetti took his first trip to Mexico since moving to San Francisco ten years earlier. After stopping in Tijuana with friends, he went south about fifty miles to Ensenada, where he stayed by himself for three days, isolated and solitary. It wasn't a pleasant trip, and he wrote, "This is the most depressing journey I have ever been on . . . I can see why Consuls drink themselves to death in towns like this, out of pure desperation. Help!" (The allusion was to Malcolm Lowry's iconic novel *Under the Volcano,* about an alcoholic British ex-consul living in Mexico.) It may seem surprising that he ever returned, but he did, and even miserable trips proved to be rich material for his writing.

NOGALES [SONORA]

1. Jack Kerouac. In his collection *Lonesome Traveler,* Kerouac writes about crossing the border from Nogales, Arizona, to Nogales, Mexico. "You can hear cantina music from across the little park of balloons and popsicles – In the middle of the little park is a bandstand for concerts,

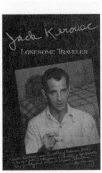

actual concerts for the people, free," he enthused. Crossing over the border into Mexico reminded him of the feeling of being dismissed from school at the end of the day. In those days, long before the drug wars of the twenty-first century, Jack wrote, "There is no 'violence' in Mexico, that was all a lot of bull written up by Hollywood writers."

CHIHUAHUA [CHIHUAHUA]

1. Allen Ginsberg, Peter Orlovsky, and Gregory Corso. Following an exhausting Kerouac Conference that Allen Ginsberg had organized and hosted at the Naropa Institute in the summer of 1982, he decided to take a short vacation in Mexico. He and Peter Orlovsky drove south in their Volvo, and Gregory Corso went along for the ride; their goal was to enjoy a relaxing getaway with a slow pace. In Chihuahua they parked the car and took a train to the town of Los Mochis on the west coast, passing through a dramatic lightning storm over the Sierra Madre mountains, where the sky filled with flashes, veins, bolts and glimmers of light. They enjoyed their spur-of-the-moment trip, but they had aged since their last group jaunt, and this journey didn't improve Allen's health — the spicy and salty Mexican food aggravated his already elevated blood pressure.

CULIACÁN [SINALOA]

1. Jack Kerouac. In April 1952, Jack Kerouac stopped in a small town near Culiacán, where a new friend named Enrique helped him buy opium, which they sprinkled over several large marijuana cigars. It was thanks to these local smokeables that Jack had his first visions in which he realized that "the earth is an Indian thing," a phrase he often repeated.

SABINAS HIDALGO [NUEVO LEÓN]

1. Jack Kerouac. On the final road trip in *On the Road*, Jack Kerouac writes about driving into Mexico and checking the map after they crossed the border at Nuevo Laredo. The first sizable town that he and Neal Cassady would come to would be Sabinas Hidalgo. Jack wrote,

"The main street was muddy and full of holes. On each side were dirty broken-down adobe fronts. Burros walked in the street with packs." In spite of its extreme poverty, they loved the place, where there were plenty of people to meet and girls to chase.

MONTERREY [NUEVO LEÓN]

1. Jack Kerouac. In *On the Road* Jack Kerouac and Neal Cassady drove south through the high country until they saw the industrial city of Monterrey in the distance, sending "smoke to the blue skies with their enormous Gulf clouds written across the bowl of the day like fleece." Approaching Monterrey was like driving into Detroit, Jack thought. He wanted to stop, and they debated whether to do so, but as usual Neal wanted to stay on the road and keep moving.

On a July 29, 1955, trip to Mexico on his own, unhampered by his restless friend, Jack found his phlebitis acting up. He stopped to buy penicillin in Monterrey and ended up spending the night here, but he decided not to pay even forty-eight cents for a skid row hotel, and instead walked the streets and slept on a park bench. In the morning he checked out the churches, old and new alike, before setting out for Mexico City.

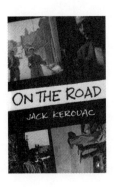

LIMÓN [TAMAULIPAS]

1. Jack Kerouac and Neal Cassady. "And suddenly Limón appeared before us, a jungle town, a few brown lights, dark shadows, enormous skies overhead, and a cluster of men in front of a jumble of woodshacks – a tropical crossroads." Jack Kerouac wrote this description of Limón in the final pages of *On the Road*. He and Neal Cassady were exhausted from another of their nonstop excursions, but it was too hot to sleep, even though they had pulled the car into a back street for just that purpose. Jack settled in, became enveloped in the atmosphere of the swamp, and watched over Neal as he slept.

SIERRA DE NAYARIT [NAYARIT]

1. Philip Lamantia. In 1955, Lamantia traveled north from Mexico City to stay in the rugged Sierra de Nayarit for several months with the Cora Indians, intent on exploring their syncretic religion in which indigenous gods and goddesses blended smoothly with Christian figures. While here, he witnessed an important *yahnah* (tobacco ceremony), shortly after which he nearly died from a poisonous scorpion bite, which resulted in intense, transcendent visions.

GUADALAJARA AND BARRA DE NAVIDAD [JALISCO]

1. Denise Levertov. The poet Denise Levertov, though not a member of the Beat Generation herself, was friendly with many of the Beat writers and often invited them to visit her during their travels. She and her husband, Mitch Goodman, lived for a spell in Guadalajara during the 1950s and had a house near the beach in Barra de Navidad. In November 1956, Allen Ginsberg, Gregory Corso, Peter Orlovsky, and his brother Lafcadio stopped over on their way from Los Angeles to Mexico City. Denise let them camp out on the floor of her South Sea–style apartment, which had a small balcony overlooking the Pacific Ocean. Allen affectionately described her as "a pigtailed gap toothed busy crazy mother who mutually digs and knows

Denise Levertov and
Allen Ginsberg

William Carlos Williams and writes fine poems with ellipses and fine phrases too." She gave them a tour of the town markets and provided a picnic on the rim of La Barranca de Huentitán, an enormous canyon not far from town.

Robert Creeley visited Levertov during the Christmas holidays in 1956. He describes his first harrowing bus trip to Guadalajara in detail in his fictional "Mabel: A Story." Creeley found a cheap hotel that was miles from Guadalajara in Barra de Navidad, right on the beach, but the windowless room had nothing but a dirt floor and reminded him of a burial crypt. He wrote that it was a "high-ceilinged one room, hotel, fly circling old light bulb hanging from traditional center of frayed cord." Here he read Beckett's *Malone Dies* and said that he had finally discovered he understood it completely.

Levertov's own works are clearly influenced by her experiences here. In her poem "The Sharks" she writes about something she must have witnessed at the beach:

> Well then, the last day the sharks appeared.
> Dark fins appear, innocent
> as if in fair warning. The sea becomes
> sinister, are they everywhere?
> I tell you, they break six feet of water.

In 1977 Levertov's mother passed away in Mexico and it inspired her to write a poem, published as part of "Five Poems from Mexico."

The heart
of Mexico sits in the rain
not caring to seek shelter,
a blanket of geranium pink drawn up
over his silent mouth

She and Mitch lived in Guadalajara until August 1957, at which time they moved to Oaxaca. They stayed in Mexico for about two years.

2. Lawrence Ferlinghetti. On several occasions Lawrence Ferlinghetti visited Guadalajara. Once in March 1969 he sat in the main plaza in front of the church, and remarked that a new avenue had been built right through the middle of the plaza since his last visit ten years before. A bus passed through, "full of dark workers, mostly Indios . . . its destination-sign reading REVOLUCION DIRECTO." Definitely an intriguing goal for a politically minded poet.

3. John Hoffman. Very little is known about John Hoffman, a poet who died in Mexico around 1952 at the age of twenty-four. Hoffman was a friend of Philip Lamantia, Allen Ginsberg, and Gerd Stern. In 1955 during the famous Six Gallery reading in San Francisco, Philip Lamantia chose to read Hoffman's poems instead of his own. Ginsberg, who famously read "Howl" that night, included references to Hoffman in lines like: "who got busted in their pubic beards returning through Laredo with a belt of marijuana for New York," and "who disappeared into the volcanoes of Mexico leaving behind nothing but the shadow of dungarees and the lava and ash of poetry . . . " The latter appears to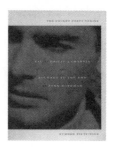

be sadly true about Hoffman. Because so little is known about him it is very difficult to pair any actual locations with John Hoffman. Some sources say he was stricken with paralysis in Puerto Vallarta in 1952 and died in a hospital in Guadalajara. Others say that he was found dead of exposure after taking drugs on a beach in Zihuatanejo. He may have died of polio or even mononucleosis. In *The Dharma Bums* Kerouac speculates that he may have poisoned himself by eating too much peyote in Chihuahua. The location of his grave is also unknown, and his body may have even been cremated. Not much has ever been confirmed, but his only book of poetry was finally published by City Lights in 2008 as part of the volume *Tau by Philip Lamantia and Journey to the End by John Hoffman*.

SAN MIGUEL DE ALLENDE [GUANAJUATO]

1. Neal Cassady. With his friend George Walker, Neal Cassady moved to San Miguel de Allende early in 1967. Here they stayed with two sisters, Kathy and Anne Van Leeuwen, in their apartment. After a short trip north to California and Oregon, Neal returned to San Miguel, this time to live with his girlfriend Janice Brown. On the night

Neal Cassady, 1964

of February 3, 1968, Cassady left her house intending to walk along the railroad tracks to the next train station. The following morning his body was found alongside the tracks. The official report was that he died of exposure, although he had been taking drugs at the time. Neal's death, followed the next year by Kerouac's, signaled the end of an era.

2. Allen Ginsberg. In June 1954, Allen Ginsberg visited San Miguel de Allende after his long stay in the jungles of Chiapas. The town was already well known as an artist's colony full of foreigners and students. Here Allen met a young painter and was glad to have some sexual contact again, his first in six months. He stayed in town for three days reading John Clellon Holmes' novel *Go,* which had just been published. Then he took a bus to see the mummified corpses in the catacombs at Guanajuato. This trip inspired a section in part two of "Siesta In Xbalba."

3. Lawrence Ferlinghetti. In March 1969 Ferlinghetti spent time in San Miguel, recording his impressions in *The Mexican Night.* He watched the Conchero dancers perform in the dusk on the main plaza in front of the seventeenth-century cathedral **La Parroquia**. He also described the unusual house where he stayed: it was a "semi-ruin of a house at **27 Recreo**, San Miguel. A *criada* (a house maid) was killed in this room when the old wood & stone roof fell in a few years ago." The rubble had been cleared, but the roof was still open to the stars when Lawrence stayed here, and it was furnished only with four flat stones and a stone sculpture of a woman's head.

CUERNAVACA [MORELOS]

1. Timothy Leary. In August 1960, Timothy Leary visited Cuernavaca on his fourth consecutive summer vacationing in Mexico. He stayed in the luxurious **Casa del Moros**, a Spanish-style stucco villa, and from a nearby village he obtained a supply of the sacred mushrooms that grew in the region. These were Leary's very first psychedelic mushrooms. He sampled them on August 9, 1960, sitting by the pool with friends, and before long he was having a life-changing visionary experience. Richard Alpert arrived the next day, and Leary couldn't wait to turn him on to the mushrooms, telling him that "I learned more in the six or seven hours of this experience than in all my years as a psychologist." This marked the beginning of their Harvard Psychedelic Project.

CHOLULA [PUEBLA]

1. Lawrence Ferlinghetti. On May 11, 1972, Lawrence Ferlinghetti visited Cholula. He kept a detailed journal in which he described seeing the many Catholic churches in town. They inspired him to write the poem "Carnaval De Maïz."

> In the churches of Cholula
> the bleeding Christs groan
> their Indian misericordias
> as Christian saints in cages
> wring their wood hands
> over bloodblack rosaries
> wailing & bewailing
> Great God Death
> in Churrigueresque chapels

VERACRUZ [VERACRUZ]

1. Bonnie and Ray Bremser. Ray and Bonnie Bremser fled to Veracruz in 1961. Ray had been released on bail pending his trial for armed robbery in New Jersey, and he and Bonnie decided that the odds of his being acquitted were slim. Bonnie went first with her baby Rachel, going by bus with a friend and staying at his house on the **Calle Mariano Arista**. Here she waited for Ray, who had lingered in Mexico City. She was high most of the time, and tried to make money by whatever means possible, which usually meant prostitution and drug dealing. To

[farm group with] Bonnie and Ray Bremser (seated on ground with daughter)

break the monotony, whenever she rode the trolleys she memorized the names of streets. Once Ray arrived, they often went to the beach at Mocambo to have shrimp and beer with friends, passing the historic Malecón district. Bonnie wrote in her memoir, *Troia,* "I would be all for the other end of the beach which was simply wilderness and they would stick by the commercial stand, making it on beer." When they occasionally came into some money, they had coffee at the expensive Gran Café de la Parroquia [**Valentín Gómez Farias 34**] and walked to the tip of land near Villa del Mar. For a while they stayed in cheap hotels, until they rented a house on the **Avenida Revillagigedo**. Bonnie usually supported this lifestyle with money she earned as a prostitute, all vividly described in her book.

OAXACA [OAXACA]

1. Lawrence Ferlinghetti. The beautiful city of Oaxaca was everyone's favorite, famous for its indigenous foods and crafts as well as its liberal politics. Lawrence Ferlinghetti is among the many writers who visited the city more than once. He spent a few days here in September 1968, writing in his journal, "Mad, a hole in my shoe, under the jacaranda trees and the great Indian laurels, roots still in the Ganges, in the plaza de Oaxaca.... And then at night by the circular bandstand listening to the marimba music, everyone out strolling or on the park benches in the semi-dark, the high lamps shining through the trees." During that trip he went to a nighttime student rally in front of the Science Institute of the University of Oaxaca, just off the main plaza, and listened to the fiery orations of the revolutionary speakers. (The location, on **Avenida de la Independencia at the corner of Alcalá,** currently houses the Law Faculty of the Universidad Autónoma Benito Juárez de Oaxaca.)

In 1982 he returned to Oaxaca before attending a poetry festival in Mexico City. He wanted to travel alone and wrote in his journal, "Loneliness is still a curse. Still, the people that singly wanted to come on this trip with me must understand: I have to be alone on trips like this. Or else they are not trips like this." Ferlinghetti, possibly more than any of the other Beat writers, created more poetry while he was on trips than he did at home, perhaps because back in San Francisco the demands of having a family and running a flourishing bookstore and publishing company did not allow him much time to sit and write at leisure.

2. Michael McClure. In 1962, Michael McClure and scientist Sterling Bunnell traveled into the mountains north of Oaxaca at the urging of Dr. Frank Barron of the Institute of Personality Assessment and Research at the University of California. Their mission was to find various psilocybin mushrooms to be used in his research. Here they went to the town of **Huautla de Jiménez** to meet the legendary Maria Sabina, a native curandera who spent her life guiding people in experiences with the "magic mushrooms" found in the area. McClure and Bunnell discovered five varieties of mushrooms and brought them back for experimentation. Many other vision-seekers visited Sabina in her hometown over the years, including R. Gordon Wasson, Bob Dylan, John Lennon, and the Rolling Stones. Anne Waldman modeled her poem "Fast Speaking Woman" on Sabina. She noted that the

Michael McClure, 1973

poem opens with "a kind of testimony of ritual purity borrowed from Sabina." Ferlinghetti would publish this poem in Number 33 of his City Lights Pocket Poets Series: *Fast Speaking Woman & Other Chants.*

3. Joanne Kyger. A lifelong traveler, poet Joanne Kyger found plenty to write about during her trips to Oaxaca. In her set of poems titled "God Never Dies: Poems from Oaxaca," she writes,

> Here in Oaxaca
> it's the Night of
> the Radishes
> Now I wave
> from the green
> balcony above
> the gardenia
> in my shoes
> without socks the sun
> is frankly generous . . .

PALENQUE [CHIAPAS]

1. Allen Ginsberg. In January 1954, while Allen Ginsberg was exploring Mayan ruins around the Yucatán and Chiapas, he stopped to visit Palenque, an ancient Mayan city which had recently been unearthed after nearly a thousand years. Palenque sat on the edge of one of the most inaccessible jungles in southern Mexico and was surrounded by impenetrable forests. In the era of Ginsberg's visit, few roads existed and most travel was done by canoe along the rivers that flowed down from the mountains of Chiapas. This made Palenque truly remote, and Allen marveled at the lost civilization that had built the large city. He was allowed to live in the archaeologists' camp and here he met Karena Shields, an American woman who had grown up on a giant *finca* that once included the whole Palenque site. She had returned to Chiapas after a career in the States as a minor actress. (Her credits included a supporting role in the 1930s radio broadcasts of *Tarzan*.) Although no longer wealthy, she was generous and hospitable and invited Allen to stay at her much smaller *finca* deep in the jungle.

Allen Ginsberg at the Mayan ruins in Palenque, 1954

Allen decided to accept her offer while waiting for money to arrive from home, so one morning they left the Palenque ruins and hiked to her plantation, nestled at the base of **Don Juan Mountain**. Her guesthouse was a large open-sided thatched-roof hut that had a central fire for heating coffee, and food was served communally. The hut and fire were tended by an Indian woman who helped Allen string his nine-foot hammock across the room.

The warm tropical climate agreed with Allen, and he ended up staying with Karena for several months. He explored the shallow river that ran through the forest not far from the house, and here he discovered a plant with heart-shaped leaves that inspired him to write a love song to Neal Cassady called "Green Valentine Blues." He swam in crystal clear mountain pools, and at night took a bottle of rum to some nearby Mayan ruins to watch the moon rise over the mountains. On some nights they'd go fishing with long spears to catch giant crawfish the size of lobsters, a regional delicacy. Most of his time he spent lying sideways in his hammock, reading and writing in his journal. The isolation was not wasted, for Allen worked five to ten hours a day writing poems, among them "Siesta in Xbalba," which he considered his best poetry to date. The first part of the poem was written while on the *finca,* and it wove together all of the Maya lands he had visited. The second part was composed later and dealt with Allen's departure from Mexico. The central theme of the poem was Xbalba, both a real geographic area centered around Don Juan Mountain and Palenque, and also an imaginary area, the place of limbo or obscure hope, a sort of Mayan purgatory/hell. Meanwhile Allen had run out of money entirely, and Shields was of little help, since she was as poverty-stricken as he was. They tried with no success to pawn her old camera to raise travel money. Finally she received some cash from the States, and in May she was able to lend Allen enough to hit the road again. He took a train to Coatzacoalcos, then a bus to Veracruz, and finally made it to Mexico City.

YAJALÓN [CHIAPAS]

1. Allen Ginsberg. Certainly one of the oddest adventures that Allen Ginsberg ever had occurred in this region late in March 1954. While he was staying on Karena Shields' remote plantation near Palenque, an earthquake struck Chiapas, centered near the mountain town of Yajalón. Before long, reports began to arrive that the whole town had been destroyed. It didn't take Allen long to realize that he might be sitting on a newsworthy story (maybe even as big as the eruption of the volcano Paricutín in a cornfield, which had attracted international attention a decade earlier). Allen decided to mount an expedition into the mountains to search for the epicenter of the quake and to witness the true extent of the damage. He flew in a tiny 1914 biplane to Yajalón, then a sleepy village of about seven thousand inhabitants. It had not, in fact, been demolished. A mountain called La Ventana rose like a wall 7,500 feet high on the south side of town, and beyond that lay Acavalna Mountain, where the tremors may have been centered. Receiving Allen as though he were a visiting geologist, a large group of men gathered to escort him up the mountain trail. They went to a giant, unexplored cavern in the side of the mountain, where aftershocks had dislodged giant stalactites from the cave's ceiling. However, there was no sign of any volcanic activity, and when Allen got back to Yajalón, he was treated like a hero for reassuring the populace on this count. He failed to spark any interest in the event from the U.S. press, however, since there was no mass destruction to offer them.

LERMA [CAMPECHE]

1. Charles Olson. In 1951 Charles Olson was living in a house in Lerma, a fishing town on the Yucatán peninsula near the larger city of Campeche. It overlooked the blue waters of the Caribbean, and Olson spent a good deal of his time writing here. For a while, when his friend Robert Creeley was looking for a place to live, he considered moving to Lerma too, but in the end he decided on France instead.

MÉRIDA [YUCATÁN]

1. Allen Ginsberg. On Allen Ginsberg's first trip alone to Mexico, he flew from Cuba to Mérida, ar-

Photo Courtesy of City Lights Archive

Charles Olson, 1957

riving on New Year's Day, 1954. After being disappointed with Cuba, he immediately found everything in Mexico to be magical. At the airport he met two Indians who offered to take him around the city in a horse carriage for just a few pesos. By chance they ran into the mayor's brother, and he invited Allen to the town's New Year ceremonies at the City Hall [**El Ayuntamiento**], complete with free sandwiches and beer served on the balcony overlooking Mérida's large central plaza, the **Plaza Grande**. While in town he stayed at the Casa de Huéspedes Hotel [**Between Calle 63 and 65 Calle 62 507**].

CHICHÉN ITZÁ [YUCATÁN]

1. Allen Ginsberg. One of the first great Mayan ruins that Allen Ginsberg visited on his 1954 trip to Mexico was

Chichén Itzá. Friends had tipped Allen off that he could get a free room near the pyramids by presenting himself as an archaeology student. For a few pesos a day he got plentiful food from the locals and had full access to the ancient city. In the evening he was even allowed to take his hammock to the top of the tallest pyramid, where he fell asleep watching the stars, something that would be prohibited today. On occasion he ate his meals at the Mayaland Hotel [**Km 120 Ctra Mérida, Zona Arqueológica Chichén Itzá**] and socialized with the archaeologists and tourists who came to see the ruins, but at night he preferred the solitude of the tropical jungle with its chirruping insects, bats, and owls. He found some interesting stone carvings of penises and took dozens of pictures of them along with many stone skulls that had been unearthed in the ruins.

CUBA

HAVANA

1. Allen Ginsberg. At the end of December 1953, Allen Ginsberg made his first trip to Cuba. From Key West, Florida, he took the short ten-dollar boat ride across the Strait of Florida. He had been looking forward to seeing the Cuban capital, and hoped to find plenty of opportunities there for sex. Disappointingly, he found pre-Castro Havana to be pretty tame. He stayed a few nights on the waterfront in the inexpensive Carabanchel Hotel [**O'Reilly 360**], where he'd been told that the staff was competent in English, but they were not. Although he spent some time visiting tourist sites, he ended the day drinking heavily, and was glad to be on his way on the morning of December 31.

In January 1965 Ginsberg had a much more inter-

Manuel Ballagas and Allen Ginsberg in Havana, 1965

esting visit to Havana. He was invited to judge a literary contest sponsored by the Casa de las Américas [**Plaza de Revolución near Calle 3**], and at the same time to witness the positive effects of Castro's revolutionary government. On this trip he had to enter Cuba via Mexico City, due to U.S. government travel restrictions. The director of Casa de las Américas, Haydée Santamaría, escorted him around town. They visited some old forts, an alligator farm, and Hemingway's house, the Finca Vigía, which is now a museum about nine miles out of town. Allen was given a comfortable room at the Hotel Habana Riviera [**Paseo y Malecón, Vedado**], and from time to time he was able to sneak away from his chaperones and visit new friends like the young writer Manuel Ballagas. These young men showed Allen the night life in Havana's El Vedado neighborhood, where he met other writers and could talk openly over drinks. After Ginsberg and Ballagas had sex in Manuel's apartment at **Avenida de Acosta 58**, Ballagas was jailed and Ginsberg was deported from the country. Allen had been enthusiastic about the new Cuba under Fidel Castro before his trip, but what he experienced was not the freedom he was looking for. While he did get the chance to spend time with poet Nicanor Parra and editor Tom Maschler in Havana, he left with the realization that this was no socialist paradise. He summed it up to Peter Orlovsky in a letter: "Cuba is both great and horrible, half police state, half happy summer camp – mixed."

2. LeRoi Jones [Amiri Baraka]. In the summer of 1960, LeRoi Jones was invited to Cuba as a member of a delegation of black activists and artists hosted by Casa de las Américas. The trip was timed to coincide with the anniversary of Castro's first unsuccessful attempt to overthrow the Batista government at the Moncada Barracks on the 26th of July, 1953. Jones was put up at the Hotel Presidente [**Calle Calzada 110**], which he said "is hardly what could be called a luxury hotel," but the rewards of the visit were great. "The Cuban trip was a turning point in my life," Jones wrote in his *Autobiography*. In addition to noting the positive aspects of the revolution for many Cubans, LeRoi had a chance to befriend writers such as the poets Nicolás Guillén, Guillermo Cabrera Infante, and Pablo Armando

Photo by Fred W. McDarrah

LeRoi and Hettie Jones

Fernández (all associated with the publication *Lunes de Revolución*). The members of the delegation were treated as honored guests and taken to many government offices, as well as to a beach club called El Obrero Círculo, before leaving for the celebrations in the town of Sierra Maestra in Oriente province. Once home, Jones wrote an essay about his experiences in Cuba that was published under the title "Cuba Libre."

3. Lawrence Ferlinghetti. In December 1960, the same year as Jones' visit, Lawrence and Kirby Ferlinghetti also visited Havana, invited by the Fair Play for Cuba Committee. They spent a week in the city checking out the post-revolutionary scene, staying at a hotel on the Paseo del Prado. Ferlinghetti kept notes in his journal, "Dramatic waterfront in Havana – Sea beating great long seawall Northside of city – Morro Castle at one end . . . Beautiful city! Beautiful trees on the Paseo del Prado – We got hotel on Prado – $5 for two – outside our windows in hotel, the trees that line the center island of the Prado are filled with starlings. . . . We have a tiny white room with a marble balcony above the avenue and the trees. Taxis toot, birds drown them out. . . . The Capitol building itself and others on the great Plaza next to it are all floodlighted . . . as are statues." During his visit, Ferlinghetti ran into Fidel Castro by chance at a restaurant, and met with Pablo Neruda, who was staying at the Cuba Libre Hotel [**Paseo del Prado 603**], formerly called the Havana Hilton. Lawrence followed Neruda to hear him read at the old National Assembly Building. Lawrence and Kirby left Havana on December 8, and Lawrence immediately began to write his poem "One Thousand Fearful Words for Fidel Castro," as well as a prose account of his stay called "Poet's Notes from Cuba."

HAITI

PORT-AU-PRINCE

1. Lawrence Ferlinghetti. In 1960 Lawrence and Kirby Ferlinghetti went to Haiti as part of their Caribbean tour, which also included Cuba and the Virgin Islands. In the capital city, Port-au-Prince, Lawrence kept a journal that was later published as "Picturesque Haiti" in the periodical *The Journal for the Protection of All Beings*. He had never experienced such devasting poverty before, and he wrote, "The coins all read Liberté, Égalité, Fraternité. These noble savages are all absolutely equal, except for the six percent who own everything not owned by foreigners."

VIRGIN ISLANDS

ST. THOMAS

1. Lawrence Ferlinghetti. Clemence Mendes-Monsanto, Lawrence Ferlinghetti's mother, was a member of a Sephardic family that had left Portugal for the Caribbean islands centuries ago. When Ferlinghetti finally began to look for his family's roots in 1960, he was surprised to find that some members of the Mendes-Monsanto family still lived on the island of St. Thomas. In late November he and his wife Kirby came here to meet his distant relative Gladys Woods. They were taken to see the old mansion that had once been the home of Lawrence's great-grandfather and stopped at **Thatch Cay**, an island off the northern shore of St. Thomas that had been owned by his family. There he met several other distant relatives, who he said reminded him of Vikings.

GUATEMALA

LOS TARRALES

1. Robert Creeley. In the fall of 1959, Robert Creeley accepted a job as a tutor for the children living on a large coffee *finca* in Los Tarrales. Since those days, the plantation has become part of **Los Tarrales Reserve**, one of the best bird-watching preserves in Central America. It is near Lake Atitlán and the volcano of the same name, a three-hour bus trip from Guatemala City. Creeley, along with his wife, poet Bobbie Louise Hawkins, and their kids, were given a house that was surrounded by tropical foliage and infested with insects of every variety. One day they found an ocelot in the living room. At first Robert was treated suspiciously by the *finca* foreman, Tito Bressani, who thought him an untrustworthy beatnik. As a result Creeley initially felt it may have been a mistake to come to Guatemala. As time passed, things improved, and Bob enjoyed teaching the children. Although the country was in political turmoil, he did his best to avoid involvement in politics. During the two years he spent here, Creeley managed to do a good deal of writing and completed much of his novel *The Island*. He also spent considerable time looking for his next job, and finally, in late April 1961, he headed north once again for New Mexico.

GUATEMALA CITY

1. Ray Bremser. Poet Ray Bremser was in prison in New Jersey, first in Trenton State and then in Rahway, from the fall of 1961 until the end of 1965. Once he was released and had finished his probation period, he and his wife Bonnie returned to Latin America, traveling through the Yucatán and Belize to settle for a time in Guatemala. Their second daughter, Georgia, was born on this trip in June 1967. It wasn't long before the couple separated, and in 1969 Ray moved back to the United States. Though written in New York in 1970, Bremser's "Black Is Black Blues" is filled with allusions to their Guatemalan life.

> tomorrow off to Atitlán
> & stuporfaction pants to
> doff, un-don, remove & all   up-
> beat the fast fat frenzy . . .

NICARAGUA

MANAGUA

1. Allen Ginsberg. On January 21, 1982, Allen Ginsberg flew to Managua, Nicaragua, to take part in the Rubén Darío Festival. He was invited as the guest of his old friend, poet Ernesto Cardenal, who had been made Minister of Culture under the Sandinista regime. Russian poet Yevgeny Yevtushenko was also invited, and together the three poets composed a prose statement which they called the *'Declaration of Three' to World's Writers*. Their aim was to show unity on an artistic level, proving that communist, capitalist, and Sandinista writers could coexist peacefully, even if their governments had a hard time doing so. The statement was widely distributed in the U.S. press. On January 25, while sitting in the bar of the Intercontinental Hotel [**Paseo de la Unión Europea**] in Managua, Ginsberg composed his poem "The Little Fish Devours the Big Fish" and set it to music.

Four years later, in January 1986, Ginsberg returned to Managua once again to take part in that year's festival.

Allen Ginsberg with Sandinista soldiers, 1982

On that trip he witnessed first-hand the negative effects of the American embargo and sanctions upon the Sandinista government and their people. He read with Jose Coronel Urtecho, Pablo A. Cuadra, Carlos Martínez Rivas, and Ernesto Cardenal. On both occasions he toured the country and saw as much as he possibly could in a short span of time.

2. Lawrence Ferlinghetti. In January 1984, Lawrence Ferlinghetti took his turn as a guest at the Rubén Darío Festival. He asked his friend, the photographer Chris Felver, to accompany him to document the trip. Lawrence himself kept a journal, which he published as the book *Seven Days in Nicaragua Libre.* By this time the Sandinista government had been in power for five years, and Ferlinghetti spent the week observing the conditions in the small socialist country. His reading took place in a theater at the **Plaza Pedro Joaquín Chamorro**, but this was only a small part of his

Ernesto Cardenal, 1990

visit, during which Ernesto Cardenal escorted him to new sites each day. They stopped in the newly built resort of **Pochomil** on the Pacific coast; in **Granada**, Cardenal's hometown on the shores of Lake Nicaragua; at **Peñas Blancas** on the Costa Rican border, where Ferlinghetti saw signs of recent battle with Contra forces; and they even visited a prison. They also took a boat out to **Solentiname**, a small island in the middle of Lake Nicaragua where Cardenal, who was a priest, had built a chapel and organized a contemplative religious community with revolutionary sympathies.

Lawrence Ferlinghetti returned to Nicaragua once more, this time for a month in the summer of 1989, bringing his son Lorenzo with him. Here they took part in the celebrations in Managua that marked the tenth anniversary of the overthrow of the military dictator Anastasio Somoza Debayle.

PANAMA

PANAMA CITY

1. William S. Burroughs. In July 1951, William S. Burroughs and his young friend Lewis Marker flew to

Panama City from Mexico City on the first leg of a longer journey. On their layover they visited a cabaret called El Ganso Azul (The Blue Goose). From here they took another plane to Quito, Ecuador, in search of hallucinogenic drugs. In 1953, after he had killed his wife, Joan, in a game of William Tell gone terribly wrong, Burroughs returned to Panama City, hoping to find asylum somewhere in South America. When he reached Panama, William came down with a case of hemorrhoids which necessitated a short stay at the American Hotel while he had treatments. In "I Am Dying Meester?" Burroughs used this cut-up: "That's Panama – Nitrous flesh swept out by your voice and end of receiving set – Brain eating birds patrol the low frequency brain waves – Post car waiting forgotten civilians 'and they are all on jelly fish, Meester – Panama photo town – Dead post card of junk.'" Burroughs also remarked on the shoddiness of this city where he couldn't get pure drugs, writing to Allen Ginsberg, "That's Panama. Wouldn't surprise me if they cut the whores with sponge rubber."

2. Jack Kerouac. Also in 1953, Jack Kerouac passed through the canal as a seaman on board the S.S. *William Caruthers*. At the time, he was working his way back east after a trip to California. When Jack arrived in New Orleans he jumped ship and never completed the voyage, thus ruining his chances of working on any ship again.

COLOMBIA

BOGOTÁ

1. William S. Burroughs. Although Gary Snyder had been ashore in Colombia when he was working as a seaman in the summer of 1948, William Burroughs was the first of the Beat writers to spend serious time here. Early in 1953, William arrived in Bogotá, his jumping-off place on a private expedition in search of the hallucinogen called yagé. He stayed at the Hotel Nuevo Regis [**Calle 18, no. 6-09, Santafé de Bogotá**]. When he entered the country, the immigration officials mistakenly dated his entry papers as January 20, 1952, instead of 1953: this was to cause him many problems and delays. After the irregularities in his documents scuttled his first trip down the Putumayo River, Burroughs returned to Bogotá to get his papers put in order, and by the time he returned in March he had contracted malaria. "Bogotá horrible as ever," he wrote, not surprisingly. While in town he had the luck of making friends with Richard Evans Schultes, a botanist who knew a great deal about yagé. Together they made another expedition with a group of Englishmen from the Imperial Institute of Mycology, some Swedish photographers, and a few Colombian assistants.

PUTUMAYO

1. William S. Burroughs. As related in his book *The Yage Letters*, Burroughs traveled through the jungles of the Putumayo Department of Colombia looking for both the vine yagé and for people who knew about its halluci-

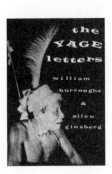

nogenic qualities. From Bogotá he went to Cali, then Popayán, Pasto, Mocoa, Puerto Limón, Puerto Asís (which he called Puerto Assis in his letters), and finally Puerto Leguízamo. On his first foray, the irregularities in his papers caused him to be detained for days in **Puerto Asís** under a casual sort of house arrest, and locked in jail for a night in **Mocoa**. Later Mocoa would be the site of his first experiment with yagé (a miserable one), and he would drink the brew again in Puerto Asís. On April 12, 1953, he was finally able to write back to Allen Ginsberg, "Mission accomplished. I have a crate of Yage with me." Once back in New York later that year, he shared the mysterious drug, nicknamed "the vine of death," with his friends. A decade later, Ginsberg would travel to Peru to find it for himself.

ECUADOR

QUITO

1. William S. Burroughs. In July 1951, two years before his trip to Colombia in search of yagé, William S. Burroughs and his young friend Lewis Marker arrived in Quito, Ecuador. It had been Burroughs' idea to take Marker along on a brief expedition in search of the hallucinogenic vine. He also thought that he might be able to seduce the younger heterosexual man if he had him all alone. When they reached Ecuador, Burroughs became ill, and after he recovered somewhat they took a circular route around the country. From Quito they went to Manta, where they stayed in the Hotel Continental, then on to Guayaquil, Ambato, and Puyo, without finding the elusive drug. Burroughs loved the tropical country, however, and made a vow to return, perhaps on a permanent basis. He wrote to Ginsberg, "Yes real jungle but surprisingly cool and comfortable where I was (2000 ft.). Unbelievably beautiful. Springs, moss, beautiful clear streams and rivers, trees up to 200 ft. high." In April 1953, he returned to Quito on his second expedition in search of yagé. This time he reported a change of opinion, "Went through Ecuador fast as possible. What an awful place it is."

PERU

LIMA

1. William S. Burroughs. On his 1953 trip in search of yagé, William Burroughs used Lima as his home base for exploring the jungle regions of Peru. He had been in Colombia for several months and traveled to Peru to learn more about the drug. One night he stayed in the Gran Hotel Bolívar [**Jirón de la Unión 958**] and pinched as much stationery from the elegant hotel as he could find for future use. After that he had to resort to more afford-able lodgings. He liked the town in general, and the boys in particular, whom he called "the least character armored people I have ever seen." On May 12, 1953, he wrote to Ginsberg, "Lima also has an extensive Chinatown, good restaurants, pleasant climate, the cheapest living I hit in South America. In short I wouldn't mind settling down here." He admired the Jorge Chávez Monument [**Plaza Jorge Chávez**], but never quite learned what Peru's most famous aviator was famous for. In fact Chávez was the Peruvian pilot who attempted to make the first flight across the Alps, only to die in a crash upon landing.

2. Lawrence Ferlinghetti. During their 1960 trip to South America, Lawrence Ferlinghetti and his wife, Kirby, headed out of Bolivia after being turned off by the destitu-tion of La Paz, taking an old steamer across Lake Titicaca to the eastern tip of Peru. They continued to find squalid conditions and poverty everywhere. Finally they arrived in Lima, where everything seemed beautiful by comparison. "Lima has a spirit and sense of being in the manner of Vienna, Paris, Madrid — one of the few cities in the entire Western Hemisphere that seems to have that certain Parisian or Continental soul," Lawrence joyfully wrote in his journal. Especially impressive to Ferlinghetti was the **Plaza de Armas** with its huge colonial buildings in the very center of the city. He wrote to Ginsberg to tip him off that he could find artists and writers hanging out at the Cafe Zella on **Plaza San Martín**.

3. Janine Pommy Vega. In June 1970, Janine Pommy Vega traveled to Peru to study the matriarchal cultures that worshiped female divinities here, as recounted in her book *Tracking the Serpent: Journeys to Four Continents*. In Lima she taught a writing course at Lurigancho Men's Prison [**San Juan de Lurigancho**], known as the worst prison in the world. The money she earned afforded her another month to explore the jungles of the interior, where she, like Burroughs and Ginsberg before her, tracked down a native curandero who could administer ayahuasca (yagé). Janine found the experience enlightening: under the influence of ayahuasca she detected "a female presence everywhere – in the leaves, the trunks of trees, the drops of water."

PUCALLPA

1. Allen Ginsberg. In 1960, after Allen Ginsberg took part in a writers' conference in Concepción, Chile, he decided to extend his visit in Latin America by going to Peru. He hoped to find a local who knew the secrets of administering ayahuasca, also known as yagé. William Burroughs had tracked down the vine on his earlier trips in 1953, and had even brought samples back for Allen in New York City, but Allen wanted to experience the drug in the habitat where it was grown and used. Ginsberg spent three weeks exploring Lima before he set out for

Pucallpa, in the Peruvian Amazon. On June 6 he sampled his first yagé in Pucallpa, and returned for several more doses. "The more you saturate yourself with Ayahuasca the deeper you go — visit the moon, see the dead, see God," he wrote to Burroughs. Then he plunged farther into the jungle via an Ucyali riverboat, stopping at several small villages. He returned to New York in July, satisfied that he had found what he'd been looking for.

MACHU PICCHU

1. Lawrence Ferlinghetti. With his wife, Kirby, Lawrence Ferlinghetti stopped to see the ancient ruins of Machu Picchu during their South American travels in January 1960. The beautiful, isolated site high in the Andes inspired Ferlinghetti.

Here he penned the first draft of his poem "Hidden Door," which he dedicated, "For Pablo Neruda, on the heights of Machu Picchu." So haunting was the vision of the lost city in the mountains for Ferlinghetti that he used it as the cover photo for his 1961 collection *Starting from San Francisco*.

2. Allen Ginsberg. During his May 1960 tour of Peru, Allen Ginsberg visited Machu Picchu for a week. Once back in his room at the Hotel Comercio [**Jirón Carabaya**] in Lima, he wrote the poem "Aether," in which he included the lines:

> the millipede's black head moving inches away
> on the staircase at Machu Picchu
> the Creature feels itself
> destroyed,

head & tail of the universe
cut in two.

BOLIVIA

LA PAZ

1. Lawrence Ferlinghetti. In late January 1960, after the conclusion of the writers' conference that had
brought them to Concepción, Chile, Lawrence and Kirby
Ferlinghetti traveled through South America on their way
home to California. One of their first stops was La Paz,
and they found the city dirty, poverty-stricken, and depressing. Ferlinghetti wrote sadly that La Paz was "a miserable, mud covered, dung hole of humanity at the top of
the world, with one fine tree-lined Prado cut through and
above the sink hole city of decaying Indian beggars, con
men and German fascists."

CHILE

CONCEPCIÓN

1. Allen Ginsberg and Lawrence Ferlinghetti.
In mid-January 1960, Allen Ginsberg and Lawrence
Ferlinghetti were invited to participate in a fifteen-nation
writers' conference at the University of Concepción. Allen
wasn't able to get a free plane ticket for his companion
Peter Orlovsky, but Ferlinghetti's wife Kirby's ticket was
paid for. All of the other writers at the conference were
from Latin American countries, and the central topic of

conversation was Castro's recent takeover of Cuba, which the Latin Americans all endorsed. The conference turned out to be a bit too heavy on politics for both Ginsberg and Ferlinghetti — in fact, they discovered it had been sponsored by the Communist party, which Allen and Lawrence had been unaware of when they accepted their invitations. One day they were taken to visit the **Lota Coal Mines**. There they saw the incredible suffering the miners underwent as they were forced to labor under miserable conditions in mines dug deep beneath the sea. It made a greater impression on them than any of the conference speeches ever could have. In a subsequent interview with the press, Lawrence answered every question posed to him with the phrase "the coal miners' faces at Lota." Ferlinghetti's great poem "Hidden Door" was based in part on his experiences at Lota.

Ferlinghetti left Chile immediately after the conference, but Ginsberg stayed on in Concepción with the Chilean poet Nicanor Parra, who offered him the use of his home for a few days. At the end of January, Allen took a train south to Temuco, visited the Isla de Chiloé, then went on to Valdivia before resting for two weeks in Calbuco. It was the beginning of an important six-month stay in South America, during which Allen searched for and found the mysterious drug yagé that Burroughs had described a decade earlier.

POSTSCRIPT

This is not the end of the story of The Beats Abroad. Even though the Beat Generation was formed when a small group of fledgling writers got together near the Columbia College campus more than seventy years ago, the Beats are still exerting their influence on the international literary scene both through their writings and their presence.

Most remarkable of all might be poet Lawrence Ferlinghetti, who at the age of ninety-six is publishing four new books this year (2015) and leaving on yet another trip to Paris at the time of this writing. Who knows what new adventures he'll have and what exciting stories he may bring back home?

Other writers such as David Amram, Joanne Kyger, Michael McClure, Ed Sanders, Gary Snyder, and Anne Waldman continue to travel abroad, their work often reflecting their experiences in other parts of the world. They are still in great demand for readings, and all the Beat writers, past and present, continue to inspire people worldwide. Ginsberg's poetry, for example, has been translated into more than fifty languages, and the list grows longer with each passing year. He is not alone when it comes to a growing international popularity. The Beat influence is alive and well not only in literature, but in art and music as well. College courses continue to proliferate, and Beat literature is taught in schools around the globe. On a recent trip to Rome, I was surprised to see more than a dozen copies of Ginsberg's thousand-page *Collected Poems* on the shelf of a Trastevere bookshop. They were being held for students taking a course that focused on a comparison of Ginsberg and Whitman. New collections of Beat works are issued regularly, and the centenary of the birth of William Burroughs was recently celebrated by a series of publications, conferences, and lectures. In the not too distant future, other writers will enjoy the same observances of their hundredth.

"The earth is an Indian thing," Kerouac wrote, but it might be amended now to say, the earth is a Beat thing.

ACKNOWLEDGMENTS

Many people have helped in the compilation of this guide. Among them were the writers themselves, who never wearied of my continual inquiries. A grateful author wishes to thank David Amram, Neeli Cherkovski, Diane di Prima, Lawrence Ferlinghetti, Joanne Kyger, Michael McClure, Kaye McDonough, and Gary Snyder. Before their deaths, Alan Ansen, Lucien Carr, Carolyn Cassady, Allen Ginsberg, Ted Joans, Judith Malina, Jack Micheline, Peter Orlovsky, Carl Solomon, and Philip Whalen, were always willing to answer my many questions and guide me along the correct path.

I was also lucky to count upon friends and scholars who contributed information, stories, and photographs. Among them were Gordon Ball, Ann Charters, Bill Gargan, Jack Hagstrom, Peter Hale, Bill Keogan, Tim Moran, Nancy Peters, Bob Rosenthal, Stephen Sandy, George Scrivani, John and Mellon Tytell, and Robert Yarra.

Also of considerable value were the archives of many university libraries and special collections. Those collections contained important resources such as journals and correspondence that often yielded important addresses and other valuable information. The caretakers of this information were generous in their help. Special thanks to Columbia University, New York Public Library, Stanford University, the University of California at Berkeley, and the University of Texas. And the Allen Ginsberg Trust under the leadership of Bob Rosenthal and Peter Hale has once again been generous in allowing me to use photographs from Ginsberg's private collection.

This is the ninth book I have worked on with City Lights, and as always, without their passionate interest, this book would not have been possible. Thanks especially to Elaine Katzenberger and Robert Sharrard in the editorial office, and Matt Gleeson, the editor who helped the book develop into the volume you now hold in your hands. And of course, to Linda Ronan, who designed the cover and the interior layout, kudos for her talent and competence.

And finally, heartfelt thanks to Judy Matz, my traveling companion in life. Her support and encouragement graces this and every project.

BIBLIOGRAPHY OF WORKS CITED

Ansen, Alan. *Contact Highs: Selected Poems 1957–1987.* Elmwood Park, IL: Dalkey Archives, 1989.

Baciu, Stefan. "Beatitude South of the Border: Latin America's Beat Generation" in *Hispania,* vol. 49, no. 4 (Dec. 1966) pp. 733–739.

Baker, Deborah. *A Blue Hand: The Beats In India.* NY: Penguin Press, 2008.

Bowles, Jane. *Out in the World: Selected Letters.* Santa Barbara, CA: Black Sparrow Press, 1985.

Bowles, Paul. *In Touch: The Letters.* NY: Farrar, Straus and Giroux, 1994.

Bowles, Paul. *Without Stopping: An Autobiography.* NY: Putnam's, 1972.

Bremser, Bonnie. *Troia: Mexican Memoirs.* NY: Croton Press, 1969.

Bremser, Ray. *Black Is Black Blues.* Buffalo, NY: Intrepid, 1971.

Burroughs, William S. *Everything Lost: The Latin American Notebook.* Columbus, OH: Ohio State University Press, 2008.

Burroughs, William S. *Naked Lunch: The Restored Text.* NY: Grove, 2001.

Burroughs, William S. and Allen Ginsberg. *The Yage Letters Redux.* SF: City Lights, 2006.

A Burroughs Compendium: Calling the Toads. Watch Hill, RI: Ring Tarigh, 1998.

Charters, Ann (ed.). *Dictionary of Literary Biography, vol. 16: The Beats, Literary Bohemians in Postwar America.* Detroit: Gale, 1983.

Cherkovski, Neeli. *Ferlinghetti: A Biography.* Garden City, NJ: Doubleday and Company, 1979.

City Lights Journal, no. 1 (1963).

Clark, Tom. *Jack Kerouac*. NY: Harcourt Brace Jovanovich, 1984.

Davies, Sydney R. *Walking the London Scene*. Glasgow: Grimsay Press, 2006.

Diano, Giada. *Io Sono Come Omero: Vita di Lawrence Ferlinghetti*. Milan, Italy: Feltrinelli, 2008.

Ferlinghetti, Lawrence. *European Poems and Transitions: Over All the Obscene Boundaries*. NY: New Directions, 1988.

Ferlinghetti, Lawrence. *These Are My Rivers*. NY: New Directions, 1994.

Geiger, John. *Nothing Is True Everything Is Permitted: The Life of Brion Gysin*. NY: The Disinformation Company, 2005.

Gifford, Barry and Lawrence Lee. *Jack's Book*. NY: St. Martin's, 1978.

Grace, Nancy M. and Jennie Skerl. *The Transnational Beat Generation*. NY: Palgrave Macmillan, 2012.

Hoptman, Laura. *Brion Gysin Dream Machine*. NY: New Museum/Merrell, ca. 2011.

Kerouac, Jack. *Lonesome Traveler*. NY: Ballantine Books, 1973.

Kerouac, Jack. *Mexico City Blues*. NY: Grove, 1959.

Kerouac, Jack. *On the Road*. NY: Penguin, 1976.

Kerouac, Jack. *Satori in Paris*. NY: Grove, 1988.

Kerouac, Jack. *Selected Letters 1940–1956*. NY: Viking, 1995.

Kerouac, Jack. *Selected Letters 1957–1969*. NY: Viking, 1999.

Lamantia, Philip and John Hoffman. *Tau and Journey to the End*. SF: City Lights, 2008.

Lawlor, William T. *Beat Culture*. Santa Barbara, CA: ABC CLIO, 2005.

Maher, Paul Jr. *Kerouac: The Definitive Biography*. Lanham, MD: Taylor Trade, 2004.

McNally, Dennis. *Desolate Angel*. NY: Random House, 1979.

Miles, Barry. *The Beat Hotel*. NY: Grove Press, 2000.

Miles, Barry. *Call Me Burroughs: A Life*. NY: Twelve, 2013.

Miles, Barry. *William Burroughs: El Hombre Invisible*. NY: Hyperion, 1993.

Morgan, Ted. *Literary Outlaw: The Life and Times of William S. Burroughs*. NY: Henry Holt, 1988.

Mottram, Eric. *William Burroughs: The Algebra of Need*. Buffalo, NY: Intrepid Press, 1971.

Nicosia, Gerald. *Memory Babe: A Critical Biography of Jack Kerouac*. NY: Grove Press, 1984.

Niemi, Robert. *The Ultimate, Illustrated Beats Chronology*. Berkeley, CA: Soft Skull Press, 2011.

Norse, Harold. *Memoirs of a Bastard Angel*. NY: William Morrow, 1989.

Paul Bowles 1910–1999: Catalogue of an Exhibition. Newark, DE: University of Delaware Library, 2000.

Pommy Vega, Janine. *Tracking the Serpent: Journeys to Four Continents*. SF: City Lights, 1997.

Silesky, Barry. *Ferlinghetti: The Artist in His Time*. NY: Warner Books, 1990.

Skerl, Jennie (ed.). *Reconstructing the Beats*. NY: Plagrame Macmillan, 2004.

Smith, Larry. *Lawrence Ferlinghetti: Poet-at-Large*. Carbondale, IL: Southern Illinois University Press, 1983.

INDEX

The Beat Generation in New York

A Walking Tour of Jack Kerouac's City

Edited by Bill Morgan

Set off on the errant trail of the Beat experience in the city that inspired many of Jack Kerouac's best-loved novels including *On the Road*, *Vanity of Duluoz*, *The Town and the City*, and *Desolation Angels*. This is the ultimate guide to Kerouac's New York, packed with photos of the Beat Generation, and filled with undercover information and little-known anecdotes.

The Beat Generation in San Francisco

A Literary Tour

Edited by Bill Morgan

The ultimate literary guide to San Francisco, packed with fabulous photos and anecdotes.

A blow-by-blow unearthing of the places where the Beat writers first came to full bloom: the rooms where Ginsberg wrote "Howl," site of the Six Gallery reading, Gary Snyder's zen cottage, the ghostly railroad yards where Kerouac and Cassady worked, and much more!

Beat Atlas

A State by State Guide to the Beat Generation in America

Edited by Bill Morgan

The ultimate tour guide for those interested in the Beats and their travels "on the road" throughout the United States. From Burroughs' Lawrence, KS, to Cassady's Denver —and everywhere in between—*Beat Atlas* contains a wealth of historical information subdivided by region and state for easy reference. Rich with literary lore and heavily illustrated with photos by Allen Ginsberg.